MY NEXT
PHASE

MY NEXT PHASE®

THE PERSONALITY-BASED GUIDE TO YOUR BEST RETIREMENT

Eric Sundstrom, PhD, Randy Burnham, PhD,
and
Michael Burnham

SPRINGBOARD PRESS

NEW YORK   BOSTON

Springboard Press
Hachette Book Group USA
237 Park Avenue, New York, NY 10017
Visit our Web site at www.HachetteBookGroupUSA.com

First Edition: September 2007

Springboard Press is an imprint of Grand Central Publishing. The Springboard name and logo is a trademark of Hachette Book Group USA, Inc.

The My Next Phase name and logo is a trademark of My Next Phase, LLC.

Library of Congress Cataloging-in-Publication Data
Sundstrom, Eric D.
My next phase : the personality-based guide to your best retirement / Eric Sundstrom, Randy Burnham, and Michael Burnham. — 1st ed.
    p. cm.
  ISBN-13: 978-0-446-58117-2
  ISBN-10: 0-446-58117-8
  1. Retirement—Psychological aspects. 2. Retirement—Planning. 3. Retirees—Psychology. 4. Personality and situation. 1. Burnham, Randy. II. Burnham, Michael. III. Title.

  HQ1062.S83 2007
  646.7'9—dc22   2007010154

10 9 8 7 6 5 4 3 2 1

Q-FF

Printed in the United States of America

To Mary, Linda, and Liz

CONTENTS

ACKNOWLEDGMENTS

We owe a debt of gratitude to many people who helped with this project. We thank Debra Fulghum Bruce for ably assisting with the writing. We are grateful to Michelle Howry, our editor, for expertly shaping the manuscript; to Karen Murgolo, editorial director, for leading the project; and to the team at Springboard Press for producing the book. We appreciate the guidance of our literary agent, Denise Marcil; and valuable suggestions from our partners, Rob Bratskeir, of My Next Phase, LLC, and Trace Hallowell, of Tactical Magic in Memphis. We are grateful to Ben Johnson and Brian Borgman at Tactical Magic for the graphic art, and to Jack Medoff for the wonderful cartoons he drew especially for this book.

We thank the many individuals whose stories we have retold—with new names and locations to keep their identities private. Most we reconstructed as composites of two or more individuals known to members of the writing team.

For help in developing and managing the Web site, www .MyNextPhase.com, we thank Bryan Owen, Brian Williams, and the team at Viget Labs in Falls Church, Virginia. For participation and assistance in developing the process for our business, we thank Mary Burnham, Candace Clinger, Ann Ford, Sylvi Horvath, Carla

Ivison, Beth Mayfield, Bob Perry, Susan Pohl, Charlie Shott, and Marty Yellin.

We greatly appreciate the encouragement, faith, and emotional support from many of those close to us, including Beth Sundstrom (mother of one of us); Dr. Rhoda K. Burnham (mother of two of us); friends John Hooper, Sid Baker, and Irwin Sollinger for their wise counsel; Gini Courter, Denny and Jerry Davidoff, Allan Weiman, Don Iron, Ralph Adams, Stu Tobin, Jeff Klomberg, Jack Raineault, and Tim Crager for their caring support; and the members of the Unitarian Church in Westport, Connecticut, for their fellowship.

We thank our children—Ted Burnham, Anna Burnham, Gregory Burnham, Spencer Burnham, Alexander Sundstrom, and Claire Sundstrom—for their faith in their fathers. We thank our wives, Liz Harris, Linda Hudson, and Mary Sundstrom—to whom we dedicate this book—for their skepticism, counsel, patience, and love. We have gained much in creating www.MyNextPhase.com. We hope this book helps you find fulfillment in the Next Phase of your life.

My Next Phase, LLC
353 Colonial Road
Memphis, Tennessee 38117
www.MyNextPhase.com

INTRODUCTION

What Is My Next Phase?

THE FACT THAT YOU ARE READING THIS BOOK SUGGESTS THAT YOU might be thinking about retirement. You aren't alone! The number of Americans fifty-five and older will almost double between now and 2030—from 60 million today to more than 107 million in 2030—as the boomer generation ages. Retirement once meant a few years of rest and relaxation. Today, in this age of modern medicine, Americans who reach sixty-five can expect to live an average of nineteen more years. By the year 2050, an estimated 40 percent of sixty-five-year-olds will reach age ninety.

So what will you do in your years of retirement—or what we call the Next Phase of life? Maybe you'd like to leave your nine-to-five job for a life without deadlines. Perhaps your financial planner says you have all the money you need, and you can afford to hike the Himalayas, write the Great American Novel . . . or do nothing at all. And how will this new stage of life affect you emotionally? After all, no matter how much you want to quit your job, it likely gives you fulfillment beyond the satisfaction of a regular paycheck. While financial preparation is important, planning for the emotional side of your Next Phase ultimately determines the success of your retirement.

This book and our interactive Web site, www.MyNextPhase .com, both grew out of a personal quest that began in 1999, when founder and CEO Michael Burnham sold a successful family business. With money no longer a primary concern, and uncertain of what he wanted to do next in life, Michael, a CPA with years of experience in business and marketing, searched for a book or program to give him guidance. Finding none, Michael sought help from organizational psychologist Eric Sundstrom, PhD (Michael's executive coach), and clinical psychologist Dr. Randy Burnham (Michael's brother). Eric, a professor at the University of Tennessee and a private consultant, specializes in organizational development, executive coaching, and personality assessment. Over the past thirty years, he has designed and conducted employee attitude surveys, training, and assessments for multinational companies such as AT&T, Exxon USA, Lockheed-Martin, M&M/Mars, and PepsiCo. Randy has run a private practice as a clinical psychologist for thirty years and has served as a trainer and professor at Northern Michigan University, Purdue University, and other institutions.

Together we found plenty of resources on financial planning for retirement—but we turned up *nothing* that offered practical assistance in figuring out what to do next in life. So the three of us decided to start a business offering personal guidance in planning for life after retirement—*non*financial planning—from a Web site. We named it My Next Phase.

Over the next few years, we questioned hundreds of people nearing or past the age of retirement. Their experiences ran the gamut from depressed to delighted. Their transitions to new phases ranged from smooth and comfortable to stressful and traumatic. Our own experience led us to look closely at individual differences. Eventually we reached this key insight: *success in retirement comes from self-understanding.* Those who become aware of their personalities can plan effectively for emotional fulfillment in retirement.

Those who don't make plans that suit their personalities risk failing at retirement.

Once we grasped the fundamental importance of personality, we began building a personality-based approach to guiding people through the transition to retirement. After much trial and error and many revisions, we devised an innovative step-by-step, patent-pending process for creating a personal plan for a satisfying future.

In this book we'll help you understand yourself and what you want for your future. We offer a series of quizzes on the seven personality traits most critical to your success in retirement. We provide exercises to assist you in gauging the amount of change in your life, discovering what has given you fulfillment in your career, identifying emotional blind spots that might lead you to fail at retirement, and using your personal style to smooth your way to a plan for your best retirement. We guide you in identifying, exploring, and selecting options; converting your best options into the ingredients of a fulfilling future; and creating a plan to test-drive your Next Phase.

We will guide you in examining your life, perhaps as you never have before. Some of what you learn about yourself here will confirm what you already know. Some may prove so revealing that it could profoundly change the way you see your future.

We believe that retirement is similar to navigating a challenging river. A few retirees may succeed by chance. However, the great majority will experience unnecessary difficulty because they set out unprepared. Some will be unsuccessful and drown in anxiety, boredom, or weariness. *My Next Phase* offers you a bridge across that river.

So what's next for you? No single answer applies to everyone when it comes to choices about retirement. In fact, what worked for your colleague, neighbor, parent, or sibling might not work for you at all. This book provides you with the tools you need to plan your Next Phase to fit *your personality*. Please read on, learn more about yourself, and let us help you create your best retirement.

PART I

Understanding Retirement

CHAPTER 1

Are You Ready to Retire?

Take the Up-4-Retirement Quiz

RON'S HOMECOMING

Do you know someone like Ron, so devoted to his work that he finds time for little else in life? For years his job was the center of Ron's life. Yet after two decades as a production manager at an auto parts factory, Ron made a surprise announcement at a company picnic: he would retire at age sixty-two. "My wife and I have decided to have some fun. We'll play golf, enjoy our leisure time, and relax."

Many in Ron's department didn't expect him to retire so soon. A gregarious, outgoing manager, they saw him walk the production line most days. He had a stated goal of speaking to everyone he supervised. "Hands-on Ron," they called him, as he made a point of knowing about every job—and of freely sharing that knowledge.

But sometimes Ron's energetic approach to supervision struck his coworkers as overly directive. "I'll never forget the day Ron called a staff meeting at eight a.m. to brainstorm new solutions for our production delays," Fred, a parts supervisor and Ron's golf buddy, said. "A dozen supervisors gathered in the small conference room and listened to Ron's solutions. He asked for ideas and took notes, and then made all the decisions himself. Ron never learned to delegate! He makes his job harder than it needs to be."

Never much of a team player, Ron showed his independent style at home, too. His wife, Jill, told her sister, "Sure, we talked about retiring. But that was only *after* Ron had told his boss that 'we' would retire in June. I couldn't talk him out of it. What'll he do without his work? I know Ron will soon get bored."

The first few weeks of retirement lived up to Ron's dreams. He continued to rise at dawn for coffee with Jill and read the newspaper and sports magazines. After breakfast Ron met friends at the city golf course for eighteen holes or went to a sports bar. On rainy days a retired neighbor would drop by to chat and join Ron watching ESPN.

Jill continued her life as usual, walking daily at the Y, volunteering at the science museum, and fund-raising for United Way. As she predicted, within six weeks Ron showed signs of boredom, resumed smoking, and acted depressed. Jill saw his mood change after Fred canceled a Saturday golf outing at the last minute. Ron told Jill he overheard Fred telling another employee, "Hey, I'm not obligated. He's not my boss anymore." Ron felt hurt and rejected, and quit calling Fred for golf.

Over the next month, Ron had more trouble finding golf partners. He called colleagues and work friends only to find them busy. With few friends to talk to, Ron soon lacked the energy he had at work. He began sleeping late and missing morning coffee with Jill. Ron skipped shaving some days. His smoking escalated to two packs a day.

With too much time at home and too little to do, Ron turned his attention to Jill. He tried to organize grocery shopping and dinner menus. He made a new budget and pressed Jill to go over it with him. When Jill showed no interest, Ron got angry. They argued. Ron remained upset the whole day.

"I knew this would happen," Jill told her sister. "He's gone from supervising employees to micromanaging me!"

Ron clearly failed at retirement. What went wrong for him? Like many others we've met, Ron didn't plan beyond his finances. He didn't understand that with his extroverted personality, he gained energy from interacting with people. Ron needed pursuits that gave him the kind of companionship and face time his job provided. He also remained unaware of how much he depended on his work for a sense of purpose in life, his reason to get out of bed in the morning.

"I told him to do something with the rest of his life three years ago and I haven't seen him since."

JEANNE'S SATISFYING NEXT PHASE

Unlike Ron, Jeanne, a former English instructor at a community college, made an effort to understand herself and to identify what gave her fulfillment before starting a new phase of life. With few debts, Jeanne lives on a modest pension and monthly Social Security checks, and owns a home in a quiet neighborhood where she can walk most places she goes.

Now fully retired, Jeanne has more time for her passion: writing. Her new novel even attracted the interest of a publisher. "I started the novel more than a decade ago, but I kept tucking it away. I stayed so busy grading papers and preparing lectures that I could never find enough time for it. Now I can finally make it my focus."

When asked about a typical day, Jeanne replied, "Most mornings I write. Some afternoons I tutor a few English students for extra income. And I find great satisfaction giving classes in English to Spanish-speaking immigrants who attend my church."

Jeanne taught college English for thirty-five years and loved every moment. In considering retirement, she regretted the thought of giving up the personal contact with students and colleagues. Then, a few years before she decided to retire, Jeanne heard that her church had started an outreach program and needed teachers to assist immigrants. She saw a special opportunity to give back to her community.

The Spanish culture intrigues Jeanne, and last year she saved enough to visit her niece studying abroad in Barcelona. She also started mentoring a young teacher at the community college who moved to the United States recently from Madrid.

Jeanne looks forward to her future with confidence, knowing she has chosen satisfying pursuits that promise personal fulfillment for years to come: writing, teaching, and giving back to her community.

THINKING ABOUT YOUR NEXT PHASE

Ron's unsuccessful homecoming contrasted sharply with Jeanne's satisfying Next Phase. By *Next Phase* we mean a new stage of life reached after ending valued activities or commitments—for many of us, this means transitioning out of the standard nine-to-five job that's given our lives structure for the last forty years or so. Adjusting to the change, and beginning new pursuits that fit your circumstances and personality, is the key to a successful Next Phase of life. With self-awareness and careful planning, you, too, can enjoy an emotionally fulfilling Next Phase, and create your best retirement.

If you belong to the baby-boom generation (born 1946 to 1964) as we do, you've experienced with us some of the changes that took us into the earlier phases of our lives: graduating from college in the sixties, seventies, or early eighties and starting full-time jobs; getting married; and having children. Of course we'll soon have to decide what we'll do in our own Next Phases as we near the traditional age of retirement. Yet while retirement used to last for only a few years, forecasters now predict life spans that reach the mid-eighties in the next few decades, with many people living to age one hundred or older. This dramatic increase in life span makes retirement planning more important than ever.

What comes to mind when someone says "retirement"? Do you think of your savings, your 401(k), your company pension, or a paid-off mortgage? Those are all important . . . but contrary to popular belief, a solid financial plan does *not* guarantee a satisfying retirement! In our work with dozens of organizations, we've seen too many people step from satisfying careers into well-funded dream retirements—only to wake up after a few months and notice something missing . . . something deeply emotional and personal.

The *missing something* naturally differs from one person to the next. Some miss the times they've spent with coworkers in the break room. Others yearn for the structure of a regular schedule, or the time alone with their thoughts while commuting. Many miss friends, families, and neighbors after selling their homes. Most miss the satisfaction they've felt from making a difference in somebody's life—even just a small difference.

We've seen many people spend years preparing financial plans for retirement, yet fail to consider what will give their lives meaning after they leave work. Even with financial freedom, after a few weeks of rest and relaxation, these men and women soon feel rudderless and confused about their remaining decades. We've also seen people with small nest eggs who mistakenly assumed they had few options, in view of their finances, who ended up depressed and unhappy.

Why? Because success in retirement has little to do with the size of your nest egg . . . and everything to do with finding emotionally fulfilling pursuits that match your circumstances and personality.

Our years of research and experience consistently reinforce one simple idea:

Personality holds the key to success in retirement.

Personality consists of *the unique combination of preferences and habits you had as a child and learned while maturing.* Among other things your personality reflects what energizes you and how you process information, make decisions, manage stress, and maintain relationships. Together, these traits powerfully determine what fulfills you now and what will sustain you later.

Our experience shows that anyone who leaves a lifelong career without fully considering his or her personality risks failing at retirement. Yet many individuals jump into retirement with no more planning than they might give a summer vacation. Within months they feel miserable and unfulfilled—and their feelings have *nothing to do with money.* Success in retiring depends on having a financial plan that supports a *nonfinancial plan* for the next phase of life—a plan that suits your personality.

"I'm financially fit, but physically I'm a wreck."

We've written this book to help you create the nonfinancial plan you need to avoid failing at retirement. Or, if you've already failed, to help you learn from the experience and make another plan for your Next Phase that suits you better!

Before we introduce our personality-based approach to preparing for your Next Phase, we invite you to assess your own readiness for retirement.

UP-4-RETIREMENT QUIZ

To see how ready you are to retire, read each statement below and mark it true or false, depending on your understanding at this moment.

True **False**

❏ ❏ 1. I feel confident that I have the financial support needed for retirement.

❏ ❏ 2. I understand my own personality well enough to make choices in life that suit my disposition.

❏ ❏ 3. I know how my personal strengths can ease the transition to retirement and how my weaknesses can make it more difficult.

❏ ❏ 4. I understand how my personality affects my relationships with those close to me (my mate, family, friends, and coworkers).

❏ ❏ 5. I have a good idea of the changes I can expect in the years ahead.

❏ ❏ 6. I'm fully prepared to cope with many difficult changes in dealing with retirement.

❏ ❏ 7. I have identified the sources of fulfillment in my life, and which sources of fulfillment come mainly from my work.

❏ ❏ 8. I have identified the sources of fulfillment I've gained mainly through my work, such as recognition, collaboration, and independent accomplishment.

❏ ❏ 9. Looking back to my youth, I have noted the activities I enjoyed most and want to try again.

True   False

☐   ☐   10. Looking to my future, I've written down the dreams I've most wanted to realize.

☐   ☐   11. I've listed many possible options for the future and selected the few pursuits that best match my personality.

☐   ☐   12. I exercise regularly for my health at least thirty minutes, three or more times a week.

☐   ☐   13. I have a strong social network of family, friends, and acquaintances outside my work or career.

☐   ☐   14. I find ways to challenge myself mentally every day, for instance by learning new things or solving puzzles or problems.

☐   ☐   15. I will continue working at least part-time after retiring.

☐   ☐   16. I have discussed with my spouse my plans concerning retirement.

☐   ☐   17. I have a clear idea of what I'll do in my Next Phase.

☐   ☐   18. I can summarize in just a few words what I intend to do in my future.

☐   ☐   19. I have chosen a role model to help guide my Next Phase.

☐   ☐   20. I have a plan for test-driving what's new in my Next Phase.

_____   My score: the number of boxes marked *true*

(A more detailed version of this quiz is available free at www.Up4 Retirement.com.)

READY OR NOT?

As you've no doubt guessed, for every statement you marked true, you indicated greater readiness to retire. If you marked the first statement true, about having confidence in your financial support, you'll feel much freer to consider options for retirement. If you marked it false, indicating financial worries, you may feel less ready to plan a new phase, though you have *even a stronger need for a non-financial plan* that involves continuing to earn. The better you understand what kind of future you hope to create, the more accurately you can estimate your financial need.

The remaining nineteen statements deal with the emotional side of retirement planning. If you haven't already counted, please go back and count how many of the twenty statements you marked true. Here's how to score yourself:

18–20 = Ready! If you marked 18 to 20 statements true, you can count yourself *ready for retirement!* (Or if you had to stretch to get to true, maybe you're kidding yourself.) For you, working through this book will mainly confirm the hard work you've already done toward planning your approach to retirement. You can expect to validate your self-understanding, gain some new ideas, maybe explore a few new options, and reinforce what you know about the coming changes in your life. You might revisit and review the main ingredients of your Next Phase, fine-tune your plans, or add new reality checks. Enjoy! You'll probably find this book a quick read and a satisfying recap of your preparation.

15–17 = Mostly Ready. If you marked 15 to 17 of the statements true, you can consider yourself *mostly ready to retire.* Statements you marked false indicate opportunities for self-insight, preparation, and planning. Working through this book will let you build on the essentials you already have in place and assist you in further exploring your approach to retirement. You can expect to enhance your self-understanding, gain new ideas, explore new options, and develop a better understanding about the upcoming changes in your life. You have a good start and will probably find this book valuable in your preparation.

10–14 = Getting Ready. If you marked 10 to 14 statements true, think of yourself as *getting ready*. You have work to do. Give yourself time—at least as much as you'd spend planning a family vacation! On your present course, you risk a difficult transition to retirement. A little preparation can make a big difference. Working through this book will help you develop a more thorough approach to retirement. You can expect to deepen your self-understanding, gain new ideas, explore a range of new options, and create a personal plan for your future. If you have started a plan, you might revisit and review the main ingredients of your Next Phase in light of what you will learn. You'll find valuable assistance in preparing for retirement.

0–9 = Not Ready. If you marked 9 or fewer of the statements true, you aren't ready to retire. You've avoided or ignored the serious work of preparing for retirement. Your golden years will turn to rust if you keep procrastinating! You have yet to gauge the challenges ahead, to ready yourself for the psychological impact of the transition to retirement, or to create a plan for what's next in your life. On your present course, you risk a failed retirement. But you can still take action. You'll benefit from reading this book slowly and carefully, and doing *all* the exercises.

READY . . . BUT CAN'T AFFORD TO RETIRE?

If you believe you can't afford to retire, you're not alone. A recent survey by the Employee Benefit Research Institute reported that 52 percent of workers had retirement savings of less than $25,000; another 13 percent had saved only $25,000 to $50,000 dollars. But even if you believe you lack the funds to support retirement, it becomes especially critical for you to spend some time preparing for your future—both the emotional *and* the financial aspects.

Please understand: this book does *not* address the financial side of your retirement. You can find many excellent books and resources on that topic. As we've said, *My Next Phase* concerns the *non*financial aspects of retirement . . . the other things we need (besides a fat bank account) to have a happy, fulfilling next stage of life. In fact, the financial and emotional aspects of retirement are inextricably linked.

During your working years, you have probably saved, invested, and built assets. But as you prepare to enter a new phase of life, your focus changes from asset accumulation to cash flow. In other words, less money comes in and more money goes out! In the accumulation stage, people ask, "Do I have enough money to generate the cash flow I need to retire?" The answer depends on your plans. That's why we encourage you to use *My Next Phase* as your first step toward preparing for your future. You need a plan before you can figure out how to finance it. Once you have that plan, you can evaluate your finances and adjust accordingly. The clearer and more specific your Next Phase plan is, the more effectively you can prepare yourself financially. Our clients have found creative ways to finance plans for exciting, fulfilling new phases—including many people who mistakenly believed they couldn't afford to retire. You owe it to yourself to understand your personality, explore your options, prepare a plan for the future, and *then* take a hard look at your finances. You may be pleasantly surprised.

FIVE KEYS TO SUCCESS IN RETIREMENT

Whenever we give seminars around the country, we make a point of asking the group, "What will it take for you to say you have a successful retirement?" A few people usually quip, "Enough money." Someone might lightheartedly say, "A live-in butler." However, most participants take this question seriously and give the same response: "I want to stay healthy enough to enjoy life."

Staying healthy in retirement depends on three key factors: physical activity, mental challenge, and social connection. But a fulfilling Next Phase also requires two more: a passion, or reason to get up each morning, and a plan for your future that suits your personality. As you consider retirement, please keep in mind these five keys to success:

1. **Physical activity**
2. **Mental challenge**
3. **Social connection**
4. A **passion**, or reason to get out of bed each morning
5. A **plan** for your future that suits your personality

Key #1: Physical Activity

Medical research leaves no doubt about the benefits of regular physical exercise for maintaining a healthy weight, reducing the risk of chronic illness, and promoting well-being. Newer studies confirm that regular physical activity, including endurance or aerobic training, resistance or strength training, and stretching or flexibility exercise, may even increase life expectancy, helping you to live *longer* as well as healthier.

In the Framingham Heart Study—which followed 5,209 residents of Framingham, Massachusetts, over the past forty-six years—researchers estimated the effects of three levels of physical activity (low, moderate, and high) among adults older than age fifty. Moderate physical activity (brisk walking, stationary cycling, water aerobics) added 1.3 more years of total life expectancy for men and 1.1 more years for women. Those who engaged in high physical activity levels (jogging, spinning, aerobics) had greater increases in life expectancy: 3.7 more years for men and 3.5 for women. As an added benefit, adults who exercised at moderate or high levels also had less risk of cardiovascular disease compared with adults who exercised less strenuously (yoga, bowling, golf with cart).

Findings also show that regular physical activity, such as walking, may help delay the onset of dementia and Alzheimer's disease, a concern for most adults over age sixty. Exercise boosts blood flow to the brain to provide needed oxygen and nutrients. One study found physical conditioning related to brain waves responsible for the quick thinking normally associated with youth.

No matter what type of physical activity you enjoy—endurance exercise, strength training, or stretching for flexibility or increased range of motion—try to exercise at least thirty minutes every day. You can incorporate physical activity into your daily chores, like vacuuming, washing windows, raking leaves, mowing the yard, and walking the dog. One of our colleagues puts on a pedometer and aims for eight thousand steps per day (two thousand steps equal a mile). Steps accumulate as she shops, walks at a mall, and works out on a treadmill. Studies show that the benefit of small bursts of exercise is cumulative and can increase overall wellness. (A word of caution: check with your physician before starting a new exercise regimen.)

Key #2: Mental Challenge

Mental challenge consists of engaging activities that require active new learning, analysis, problem solving, or agile thinking—pursuits like mastering a foreign language or a musical instrument. Recent research suggests that mental activity may help maintain cognitive functioning with advancing age.

We recommend that you maintain some kind of mental challenge throughout your life. It could come from taking a class, keeping a daily journal, writing for publication, doing crossword puzzles or Sudoku, playing competitive bridge or chess, or other mentally demanding activities.

Some intriguing findings suggest that older adults who play musical instruments for symphony orchestras rarely develop Alzheimer's disease. In addition, researchers have discovered increases in cognitive performance in both healthy individuals and Alzheimer's patients after exposure to classical music.

Many of our clients choose to stay mentally active by continuing to work in their professions. Findings confirm that professionals who keep working beyond the traditional age of retirement—even part-time—tend to remain healthier than those who don't work as they age. Bottom line: find something mentally challenging to do in your Next Phase that requires new learning or mastery, preferably a personal *passion* (as discussed on page 18).

Key #3: Social Connection

Social connection includes activities with friends, family, and community that make you feel known, loved, cared for, and valued. The most important social ties involve friends, who voluntarily choose to maintain relationships with you. Research shows that people who stay connected with friends tend to live longer, healthier, and mentally sharper lives. Some research demonstrates that having supportive friends can buffer the adverse effects of stress, reduce the risk of illness, and speed recovery. Connections to a partner, family, friends, and a community may even strengthen the immune system, particularly among older adults. In contrast, the health risks from social isolation compare with those of cigarette smoking.

Lack of social support correlates with cognitive dysfunction and poor health in later life. Findings published in the journal *Lancet* reported that after following twelve hundred people in Stockholm, Sweden, for three years, researchers found that individuals with limited social networks had a 60 percent higher risk of developing dementia and Alzheimer's disease. In another finding, having a good long-term relationship at age fifty correlated with good health at age eighty.

Greater benefits flow from membership in a supportive community, a group of people who depend on one another from day to day. Community connection often means frequenting a place where the "regulars" greet you by name, acknowledge you without prompting, and miss you if you don't show up. You can find community connection at your church or religious organization, the neighborhood Y, a fitness center, a benevolent organization, and many other places.

Key #4: A Passion That Actively Engages You with Life

No matter what you plan for your Next Phase, the evidence consistently shows that you benefit from productive, active engagement with life as you age. In one study of healthy men and women with an average age of seventy-one, researchers found the highest survival rates in those individuals who had "something to get up for in the morning," whether it was a full- or part-time job or even a golf date. In another study researchers determined that the happiest retirees didn't necessarily have the most money, but had what they regarded as meaningful commitments. Other research found adults engaged in paid or volunteer work less likely than others to suffer physical or mental illnesses. In brief: active engagement brings a longer, healthier, and more fulfilling retirement.

Key #5: A Plan for Your Future—One That Suits Your Personality

Success in launching a new phase of life depends on having a plan built on self-understanding. In particular, it calls for insight into seven key personality traits linked to the critical tasks of a life transition. The better you understand your personality—how you navigate the stress of change and what you need for personal fulfillment—the more effectively you can evaluate your options for the future and plan a new phase that suits you.

YOUR NEXT PHASE

Unlike other books on retirement planning, this book focuses on *you*—your personality and emotional fulfillment—not your finances. As you read, you'll move quickly through a discussion of retirement to a series of helpful Personality Quizzes, inventories, and practical steps that enable you to learn more about what you will need for a successful Next Phase of life. Finally, you'll complete the planning template in the last chapter with simple goals for your future. You can use the resources in this book now to better understand yourself and to plan your best retirement.

This chapter began with two contrasting accounts. The first, Ron's Homecoming, repeats a common theme: people go into retirement without understanding themselves and end up failing on their first try—because they focus their attention on financial planning and overlook their sources of personal fulfillment. Fortunately Ron, and those who follow similar paths, can learn from experience and rethink retirement. The second story, Jeanne's Satisfying Next Phase, illustrates the experience we hope you have with your Next Phase: a workable plan for the future—based on self-understanding—that suits your personality.

We wrote this book to help you create a plan for your Next Phase, step-by-step through the seven key personality traits. We hope you find the experience enjoyable as well as worthwhile.

CHAPTER 2

Is Retirement History?

How Boomers Are Redefining Retirement as We Know It

THE TRADITIONAL RETIREMENT

When Jack graduated from college in 1963, he had four goals: get a good job, own a home, start a family, and eventually—like his father—retire to a life of leisure.

Jack got the job first, as a chemist for a pharmaceutical company. He bought the home in New Brunswick, New Jersey, at age twenty-six, just before marrying Helene, his college sweetheart. Jack and Helene had one child, Pete.

When Pete left for college, Jack, then fifty, bought a second home in a large retirement village near Myrtle Beach, South Carolina. Between family vacations at their beach home, he rented it out to cover the mortgage payments.

Jack and Helene prepared carefully for their retirement to the beach house. When Jack turned sixty-one, a year before he would leave his job, they put the New Brunswick home up for sale. They discussed what they hoped to do, and quickly agreed they would spend even more time playing bridge, and doubles tennis, too. "We're both big extroverts," Jack said, "so we'll want to get involved in a community group or two like the environmental organization we support in New Brunswick."

Jack and Helene began the sentimental process of cleaning out the attic and closets and going through their belongings. They chose favorite pieces of furniture and memorable possessions to take along, and gave the rest to Goodwill.

Then, exactly as planned, the week after Jack turned sixty-two, he and Helene said good-bye to friends and coworkers and drove down the Atlantic coast highway to their Next Phase, in South Carolina. On the way they stopped to visit their son and his family in Richmond, Virginia, only five hours from their beach house.

Some people who retire to a life of leisure soon get bored. Not Jack and Helene. If you don't find them playing tennis or walking the beach, try the clubhouse. Helene has probably organized another bridge party. Even though Jack seemed fulfilled with his classic retirement, when a former colleague visited last summer, he wondered if Jack missed his job.

Jack replied, "Not at all. I took my career as a chemist as far as I wanted. Now I really enjoy the chance to get serious about bridge, enjoy tennis, and spend time with our friends here. I'm too busy enjoying retirement to miss my job."

Jack and Helene's example illustrates traditional retirement at its best. This couple managed to build all five keys to success into their new phase of life. Key #1: Regular physical activity? Tennis. Key #2: Mental challenge? Duplicate bridge. Key #3: Social connection? Friends at the clubhouse and in town; visits to family nearby. Key #4: A passion? Playing bridge. Key #5: A plan that fit their personalities? They talked through what would suit two "big extroverts" and chose accordingly. Five keys out of five—clearly a success.

Jack followed a long tradition of leaving work for a retirement to leisure, which developed in the United States soon after the Depression. Many of us in the baby-boom generation saw our parents adopt the same classic style of retirement. But today, a traditional retirement to leisure—especially a successful one like this—may be more the exception than the rule.

ANOTHER APPROACH TO RETIREMENT: DON'T!

Like many baby boomers, Anne, the owner of a café near Mississippi's Gulf Coast, can't imagine giving up her work anytime soon. "After I graduated from high school, my uncle needed help at his café and offered me my first job," she says from behind the counter. "I learned everything about running the restaurant from him. Then when he got sick about ten years ago, he gave it to me."

Anne thinks of her customers as extended family. She gives them complimentary coffee and a slice of her celebrated coconut pie on their birthdays. They, in turn, bring Anne gifts from their travels and invite her to family baptisms, graduations, and weddings.

"I know the name of just about everyone who walks through that door," Anne says with pride. "I also know what's weighing on their minds, and I listen when they need to talk. Most of the time, I can tell you exactly what they want to eat."

What keeps her going? When asked why she doesn't sell her restaurant and take a rest, Anne has a quick answer: "The satisfaction I get from serving people. I'll keep cooking for my customers until the medics carry me out feetfirst!"

Anne found her life so satisfying that she felt no need to consider a new phase as she got older. Those like Anne who choose to keep working could become models for baby boomers, as studies show more people want to continue working at age seventy or beyond.

What about you? Will you join the rising tide of baby boomers who intend to keep working at least part-time? Or will you follow the tradition of a leisure-focused retirement like Jack's and Helene's at Myrtle Beach?

A Brief History of Retirement

Retirement as we know it has its roots in nineteenth-century Germany. Chancellor Otto von Bismarck, who designed Germany's old-age social-insurance program, set the retirement age at seventy, thinking few would live that long. It was a pretty safe bet—at that time in Germany, the average life expectancy was only forty-five years.

In the United States, the concept of retirement began with the Social Security Act of 1935. President Franklin D. Roosevelt launched social insurance and proposed a retirement age of sixty-five. It represented an optimistic goal at a time when the average American lived only to sixty-two. Still, for those who lived long enough, the Social Security system offered dependable financial assistance from the government.

The word retire *comes from the French verb* retirer, *meaning "to take back or withdraw." In retiring from our careers, we retreat from pursuits in which we have invested time, energy, and our senses of ourselves and our future—pursuits that have created or defined our relations with others.*

Social Security changed workers' expectations in the United States, and many began to assume that the government would support them financially in their old age. Thanks to company pensions and government programs like Social Security, older adults in the mid and latter twentieth century had more income. Many enjoyed "Golden Years" of leisure, a well-deserved reward for years of hard work. Retirement communities flourished in Florida, Arizona, and California. In 1960, developer Del Webb started Sun City, a recreational retirement community in Arizona that grew into one of the state's largest cities.

Today the concept of retirement has changed yet again, and our parents' idea of retirement could soon become obsolete. With our physically less demanding office jobs, improved health, and longer life spans, we may rethink the traditional idea of retirement as relaxation. In 1900 the United States had only 3.1 million citizens age sixty-five or older, compared with approximately 36 million (one out of eight people) today. By the middle of the twenty-first century, the proportion will shift—to an estimated one of five Americans age sixty-five or older. And these mature Americans will look very different from previous generations of retirees.

Changing Rates of Full-time Work by Men in the United States, 1880–2000	
Year	*Percent of Men in USA Older than 64 Working Full-time*
1880	*78*
1900	*65*
1920	*60*
1940	*44*
1960	*40*
1980	*25*
2000	*18*

THREE REASONS TRADITIONAL RETIREMENT COULD BECOME HISTORY

In view of the changes emerging in the twenty-first century, we see three reasons why baby boomers will probably reinvent retirement.

Reason #1: We Are Living Longer

"I'm not living my dad's retirement," Joel said. "He was forced into early retirement by medical problems. At sixty-four, my dad could barely walk up the front steps. Now I'm sixty-four and I play racquetball before going to the office each day, work full-time, and spend my summers traveling with my wife and grandkids."

"It's Jimi Hendrix. Ever hear of him?"

Not only do we have a longer life expectancy, but advances in medical science offer improved quality of life as we get older. Our generation has seen significant progress in treating degenerative diseases associated with aging, such as arthritis, osteoporosis, cardiovascular diseases, diabetes, and certain types of cancer. Improved geriatric medicine enables us to avert or postpone many kinds of disability that aging brings, and to enjoy better health through our longer life spans.

Reason #2: We Are Working Longer

In a recent poll conducted by AARP, 70 percent of baby-boomer participants said they intend to keep working part-time or never retire. If our generation carries out those intentions, we could redefine traditional retirement—from a time of leisure to a new phase of life that involves work in one way or another. More of us might choose to continue working full-time. If so, we baby boomers might reverse the trend shown in the table on page 24. Some of us might even start new careers, using our time, skills, and experience to benefit others. Or maybe instead of leaving work entirely, we might follow the example of broadcast journalist Tom Brokaw. After more than twenty years as anchor of *NBC Nightly News*, Brokaw left the show to do part-time reporting, saying he would now "do fewer things, slower."

Reason #3: We Have More Options than Ever

As some in the baby-boom generation leave the workforce, the resulting labor shortage could create new opportunities for those who want to work. The number of twenty-five- to thirty-nine-year-old workers will decline by 6 percent by the end of this decade. By 2011, when the first boomers turn sixty-five, available jobs could outnumber workers by more than 4 million. By 2031, that gap may widen to 35 million. The likely labor shortage over the next thirty years translates into a huge demand for boomers to work. According to a study by AARP, a majority of United States companies are bringing back retirees as contractors, consultants, or full-time employees, to retain the valuable knowledge and experience of their aging workforces. Our experience represents a valuable asset in the shrinking workforce of the twenty-first century.

If you're concerned that today's companies might lay off older workers first when cutting costs, you can cross that off your list of worries. Some recent Department of Labor data actually show higher rates of layoff among *younger* workers (under age forty) over the past two decades. Similarly, you can take comfort knowing that the educational gap between younger and older workers has disappeared.

But what if you don't want to work? Many boomers see their

Next Phases as opportunities to mentor the next generation, or volunteer to help those in their communities or even in foreign countries. Others see the possibilities for more education or travel to new places. Still others see chances to pursue lifelong interests or expand their hobbies. Some prefer to focus on recreational interests, such as golf, tennis, or skiing.

IF WORK IS YOUR PASSION

When Norm, sixty-three, retired and moved to his new home in a South Florida golf community, he couldn't wait to play golf—all day, every day. Yet after playing golf almost daily for six months, this former manager felt depressed. "Golf was simply not enough," Norm told friends. "Sure, trying to shoot under eighty was a great goal. After a while, though, the competition didn't mean as much. Mental atrophy set in. I lacked a real purpose in life."

Today Norm still plays golf, but not nearly as often. He and his wife, Jacqueline, opened a small art gallery in the historic district of town near the beach. Together they spend the summer months visiting family and friends and searching for new artwork to display at the gallery. During the winter season, they showcase different artists from the Southwest at their gallery and get together with new friends in their golf community.

For many people like Norm, work brings too much fulfillment to leave it behind. Some older workers like Saul, seventy-three, work part-time in their field instead of retiring. "I work about twenty hours a week for the same engineering firm I was with for almost four decades, but now I'm a consultant. I like staying connected to my work and colleagues. I still have plenty of free time and extra income to enjoy recreation and travel with my wife and family."

Maybe for you, work does not necessarily have to generate pay. If so, you might join the many baby boomers who choose to do volunteer work. Perhaps volunteering for a well-known service organization such as Habitat for Humanity or the Red Cross would suit your personal style. Maybe you'd enjoy volunteering overseas in a remote location to help impoverished people in third-world countries. If you feel passionate about an environmental or a human rights or a pro-life cause, you might find purpose in a political-action group. Some individuals thrive in religious institutions, schools, museums, or service organizations. No matter where you volunteer, research shows that volunteerism, like any outward expression of self-determination, can boost your immune system and buffer your stress response.

People who retire without some kind of active, personally fulfilling pursuit face a harsh reality: *a risk of shortening their lives.* We know cases of retirees who died early in their rocking chairs, echoing a wider trend found in research by an insurance company: businesspeople who retire to a life of leisure may reduce their life expectancy on average *by nine to ten years.* A passion, an active engagement with life, represents one of the keys to success in retirement.

According to the United Nations, the proportion of the global population over age sixty will grow to one in five by the year 2050, compared with one in twelve in 1950.

THREE REALITIES OF BOOMER RETIREMENT

Before you put serious effort into planning your Next Phase, you would have to see a need. Yet if you believe retirement means a life of leisure, you might see little reason to plan. If you see retiring as one long, well-deserved vacation from a hard job, why would you spend time considering your options? Wouldn't you just leave your job behind and enjoy your rest? If retirement planning means financial planning, and if you have enough savings, why plan further? Unfortunately, prevailing stereotypes of retirement could easily put you in a mind-set of complacency about your future.

Reality #1: Retirement Offers Much More than a Long Vacation

At sixty-five Richard retired from a General Motors auto assembly plant. He received a gold GM watch, started drawing his company pension, and devoted himself to his passion for fishing. Richard disengaged from his job. He traded a life of strenuous physical work for relaxation and leisure. Who wouldn't make the same bargain? After decades of demanding, exhausting labor, retirement to a life of leisure had to seem attractive, maybe even irresistible. The work certainly offered many sources of satisfaction—like friendship and comradeship, pride in a job well done, mastery of a craft, and opportunities to exercise influence. Even so, the long, hard decades left Richard physically worn out, mentally tired, and emotionally ready to walk away without looking back.

For employees today who don't like their jobs and find little satisfaction beyond their paychecks, retirement offers a welcome escape. The stereotype of retirement as a retreat to leisure made sense from Richard's perspective. He and others have regarded retirement as an extended vacation.

Many people approach retirement by disengaging from their jobs, with no long-term plans beyond an extended rest. But they soon discover what they miss—things about their work that gave them personal fulfillment—and find ways to reengage. For example, Naomi, sixty-one, retired from her job as a librarian in Indianapolis and moved to a cottage on Virginia's sandy coast. The isolated setting seemed ideal for the reading and writing she'd dreamed of doing. Yet after living alone at the beach for a few months, Naomi felt something missing. She remembered what drew her to her library career in the first place — the satisfaction of helping each patron find the right book. When Naomi started volunteering at the municipal library nearby, she resumed some of the pursuits in her career that she had found satisfying, and her retirement was complete.

Jack, the chemist who chose a traditional retirement at Myrtle

Beach, offers another example of a fulfilling reengagement. After he left his job, he and his wife continued doing what they enjoyed: bridge, tennis, and travel. They stayed connected with their family, community, and friends. In brief, they reengaged with life.

You can easily find role models actively engaged in their sixties, seventies and beyond. For instance, philanthropist Bill Gates, the cofounder of Microsoft and the world's wealthiest person, stepped back from the day-to-day direction of Microsoft's operations and turned to philanthropy. With financial gifts from billionaire Warren Buffett and others, the Gates Foundation became the world's largest charity with a $29 billion endowment devoted to fighting fatal diseases and improving education in the world's poorest countries.

The Harvard psychoanalyst Erik Erikson used the term *generativity* to refer to the act of continuing to make a difference. To Erikson, generativity meant mentoring the next generation and giving back to the community. The opposite, *stagnation*, involves disengagement and self-absorption, offering little to anyone.

So, what will you choose in your Next Phase? Generativity? . . . Or Stagnation? Active engagement? Becoming aware of the seven personality traits critical to a successful transition to retirement will give you the self-awareness you need to prepare for a fulfilling Next Phase.

Reality #2: Financial Planning Is Important—But It's Not Enough

Consider Laura, a financially secure stay-at-home mom married twenty-nine years to John, a commercial pilot who was gone many days on international flights. The couple decided that Laura would devote full time to managing the household and raising their three children. For most of her adult life, Laura made homemaking her career—one that gave her complete fulfillment. But after taking her youngest son to college, Laura drove alone to an empty home.

Like other homemakers whose last child leaves, Laura faced

what she called her "empty next." She and John had a dependable income and enough savings, so she did not have to work. But she wanted a sense of purpose in her life. Like some employees whose jobs end, she had no plan for her future—yet.

The United States Census Bureau estimates that the number of families with no children under age eighteen living at home will rise from 36 million in 1995 to 46 million by 2010, a gain of 28 percent in fifteen years.

In our seminars we tell participants that their financial plans provide the sixth thing they need for a successful, satisfying retirement. Of course, someone always asks, "So what are the first five things?" You saw our answer in chapter 1: the five keys to a successful retirement. Here they are again, for emphasis. To create your best retirement, you need:

1. A **plan for your future** so you know what you'll do. A plan that fits your circumstances *and suits your personality.*
2. A **passion**, or a reason to get out of bed in the morning, which gives your life meaning and offers personal fulfillment.

To enjoy the pursuits you choose, you have to remain healthy. That means building three things into your plan:

3. **Physical exercise,** ideally every day, or at least most days.
4. **Mental challenge,** a pursuit that requires sustained concentration, new learning, and active problem solving.
5. **Social connection,** with friends who choose and enjoy your company, and check on you when you don't show up.

We'll explain how to incorporate the five keys in your Next Phase later in the book. If you want help with the sixth thing, a financial plan, talk with your financial adviser. Just make sure you have a serious, thoughtful answer when your adviser asks, "So what do you plan to *do* after you retire?" You'll know after you complete your planning template in chapter 10!

Reality #3: Retirement Can Be a Tough Transition

If retirement just means leaving work for a life of leisure, you might ask, "How hard can that be?" We've asked many retirees about their transitions to retirement, and maybe a third of them say something like "A lot tougher than I expected."

RETIREMENT IS A SOLO PASSAGE

So what makes retirement difficult? For one thing, it's probably the first major life transition we face entirely on our own—our first solo passage. When you graduated from high school, the whole community watched and applauded. Family, friends, and community probably turned out for your wedding—and coached you through the adjustment to marriage. You probably got orientation, training, and mentoring on your first job. Your new coworkers taught you what you needed to know, and probably helped you over the rough spots.

Yet most retirees drive home from the retirement party with no support group in sight—no mentor, no orientation-to-retirement program. Unless, of course, you've prepared. It's up to you this time . . . *you alone.*

EVERYTHING CHANGES ALL AT ONCE

The second difficult thing about retirement—and for many the *main* thing—concerns the number of different parts of life that change all at once. If you leave your job, your relationships with coworkers change, along with everyone associated with work. You lose the status, influence, and power you once had. You lose the time structure of daily commitments, the physical workplace, the comradeship, and the daily commute. Your relationship with your mate changes as you spend more time at home. Your relationship to your home changes. Your relationship with money changes without a regular paycheck. If you relocate, add changes in your relationships with family and friends who live nearby. If you exercised at work, now you have to find a new routine. For some the list gets even longer.

Some research suggests that retirement can bring as much stress and emotional shock as divorce or the death of a loved one. Many find retirement highly stressful, even overwhelming. Others, of course, prepare in advance and have a better experience.

PREPARING FOR YOUR FUTURE

Whatever else you do as you prepare for your Next Phase, find out what gives you emotional fulfillment *before you consider retiring*. If you love your work, maybe you'll want to stay at it, or downshift. Look at veteran CBS reporter Daniel Schorr, still active in journalism in his nineties as a senior news analyst for National Public Radio. Justice Ruth Bader Ginsburg continues to work in her seventies, having served on the United States Supreme Court since 1993.

Whether you decide to do "fewer things, slower" like Tom Brokaw or go full tilt, like Ruth Bader Ginsberg, prepare in advance. In the next chapter, we'll explain the seven personality traits that determine your success. Use these traits to gain self-insight as you begin to envision a life that suits your personality. We want you to design your best retirement. It's your future—let us help you make it fit.

Great Achievements by Individuals Over Sixty

- *Sophocles wrote* Oedipus Rex *at seventy and* Electra *at ninety.*
- *Michelangelo began work on St. Peter's Basilica in Rome at seventy-one.*
- *"Grandma Moses" took up painting as a hobby at seventy-six.*

- *Laura Ingalls Wilder, author of* Little House on the Prairie, *published her first book at sixty-five.*
- *Benjamin Franklin helped write the Declaration of Independence at seventy.*
- *Mother Teresa continued her missionary work until her death, at eighty-seven.*
- *Arthur Rubinstein gave one of his greatest piano performances at New York's Carnegie Hall at eighty-nine.*
- *Golda Meier was named prime minister of Israel at seventy-one and held that office for five years.*
- *Mahatma Gandhi led India's opposition to British rule at seventy-seven.*
- *Frank Lloyd Wright completed the design for New York's Guggenheim Museum at eighty-nine.*
- *John Glenn returned to space at seventy-seven.*
- *At seventy-seven, Jimmy Carter led the launch of Habitat for Humanity.*
- *Robert Byrd, senator at eighty-nine.*
- *Katharine Hepburn starred in the movie* On Golden Pond *at eighty-five.*

CHAPTER 3

What Is Your Retirement Style?

How Your Personality Determines Your Best Retirement

WHAT WILL YOU DO ON THE FIRST DAY OF YOUR RETIREMENT?

"Here's my plan for the first day," Ed said at a My Next Phase seminar. "I will be at home, so I made a schedule for the day starting there. I'll take a morning walk with my friend, Al, first thing—then at about eight a.m., I'll have breakfast with my wife." Ed outlined the day in precise time blocks, explaining that he would include quiet time for reading along with some volunteer projects on his list.

Lynne, another participant, said, "Oh, I thought we were supposed to come up with ideas and options—you know, describe what we *could* do. I had so many different thoughts. I want to go walking on the beach, have breakfast in bed, start an herb garden, serve breakfast at a homeless shelter, read the *New York Times*. . . ."

Both Ed and Lynne were answering the same question: "What will you do on the first day of your retirement?" So why did Ed make a definite plan with a time schedule, while Lynne continued to list options and committed to none in particular?

The answer? *Personality differences.* Ed has a Structured Planning Style, and Lynne has the opposite—a Flexible Planning Style. One favors organization and closure (Structured); the other prefers spontaneity and options (Flexible).

Under time pressure, Ed acted true to his Structured style, reflecting a preference for living in an organized way. He allotted time to explore options and then sought closure. He made a schedule and decided what to do and when to do it. As Ed gave his plan, you could hear in his voice how definitely he had decided the day's itinerary: first a walk, and then breakfast. Settled.

Lynne expressed the opposite Planning Style—Flexible. Unlike Ed, Lynne didn't assume that the assignment called for a plan. On the contrary, she heard a call for ideas and options, which she gladly provided. People with Flexible styles, like Lynne, tend to prefer options, as many as possible. However, planning a schedule doesn't come as easily to someone with a Flexible style, so organizing a first day of retirement in a short time proved difficult.

Planning Style represents just one of seven pairs of opposite personality traits that hold the key to a successful Next Phase. In this chapter we'll introduce you to all seven pairs of traits, one pair at a time. We'll explain the differences associated with each pair of opposite styles, using two examples of individual Personality Profiles to illustrate the contrasting traits in each pair. Finally, we'll invite you to discover your own Personality Profile.

WHAT IS PERSONALITY ANYWAY . . . AND WHY DOES IT MATTER?

Personality consists of your individual style of planning, interacting with people, managing stress, and other personal habits and preferences that remain relatively constant over time and situations—the unique combination of traits that make you distinctly yourself.

Why does personality matter? Simply put: *who you are determines what fulfills you—and what doesn't.* For instance, if you're Outgoing, spending a long time alone at an isolated mountain cabin probably wouldn't fulfill you—because Outgoing individuals have high needs for social contact. Or if you're Independent, you might not feel fulfilled working with a team (unless you can direct the action)—because Independent people have high needs for autonomy. When you understand your personality traits, you can choose activities that fit who you are.

Personality also matters because who you are—your personality traits—determines how you make choices in life. If you understand yourself and remain aware of your personal preferences and habits, you can use them to your advantage. But if you're unaware of your habits, they can get you into trouble as you make the transition to retirement.

For example, if you take a Structured approach to planning, you might decide too quickly, like Ron in chapter 1, and spend too little time gathering information and exploring options before committing to a course of action. If you become aware that you tend to rush to judgment, you can approach your transition to retirement thoughtfully. You can discipline yourself to remain open longer, spend more time getting informed, and explore your options more fully before settling on a course of action.

Understanding your personality enables you to manage your choices about your Next Phase. If you remain unaware of your habits and preferences and don't manage them, your choices could go awry. Awareness of your personality enables you to make choices that fit for you. Unfortunately, understanding yourself takes hard work. It calls for paying attention to personal habits that have become automatic.

YOUR SEVEN KEY PERSONALITY TRAITS

The basis for our personality-based approach to retirement is a Personality Profile consisting of seven pairs of opposite traits. Understanding them enables you to choose pursuits that satisfy your personal needs.

1. Are You Outgoing or Contemplative? Your *Social Style* determines your need for face time, connection, or solitude and the kind of interaction you prefer—one-to-one or in groups.

Brain of a Baby Boomer

2. Are You Responsive or Resilient? Your *Stress Style* determines how much stress you experience from pressures and change in your life, and how you manage it.

3. Are You Independent or Interdependent? Your *Activity Style* determines your need for autonomy or collaboration—and your ideal mix of solo and team pursuits.

4. Are You Practical or Visionary? Your *Information Style* determines how you process information—by focusing more on details or the big picture, and how you see your options.

5. Are You Optimistic or Cautious? Your *Outlook Style* determines how you approach the future—by expecting the best or preparing for the worst—and how you evaluate options.

6. Are You Empathetic or Analytic? Your *Decision Style* determines your priorities in making decisions—subjective feelings and relationships versus hard facts and results.

7. Are You Structured or Flexible? Your *Planning Style* reflects your comfort with planning—whether you prefer a settled agenda or open options.

Each of the seven pairs of opposite personality traits corresponds to something you must do in your transition to retirement. To succeed you'll need to: seek future pursuits that match your social needs (Outgoing or Contemplative); manage the stress of a major life change (Responsive or Resilient); identify activities that fulfill you (Independent or Interdependent); envision your options (Practical or Visionary); evaluate your choices and pick the ingredients of your future (Optimistic or Cautious); decide which role models will guide you (Empathetic or Analytic); and prepare a plan (Structured or Flexible). To help you understand the seven pairs of opposite traits, we'll describe examples of two contrasting personality profiles: Laura's and Jeanne's.

Laura is the stay-at-home mom who, after taking her youngest child to college, returned home to an "empty next" and no plan for her future (page 30). Jeanne, the former community-college instructor, successfully retired to a life of writing and service (page 6). Later, in chapters 4 through 10, we'll give you an opportunity to take the seven personality quizzes and identify your own key traits.

1. What Is Your Social Style? Outgoing vs. Contemplative

Your Social Style determines your need for social contact—how much face time and companionship you need , how you like to interact with people, and how you gain self-insight. This personality trait can range from Outgoing to Contemplative or can be Mixed (a blend of the two).

Laura's Personality Profile

SOCIAL

OUTGOING	**MIXED**	**CONTEMPLATIVE**
Gregarious. High social needs. Multi-tasks. Thinks out loud.	Balances interaction and solitude. Reflects and talks to gain insight.	Reserved. Interacts one-to-one. Needs solitude to reflect.

STRESS

RESPONSIVE	**MIXED**	**RESILIENT**
Sensitive to change and stress. Recovers slowly. Needs support.	Handles pressure and change up to a point, then gets stressed.	Tolerates change. Calm under pressure. Handles stress well.

ACTIVITY

INDEPENDENT	**MIXED**	**INTERDEPENDENT**
Self-directed. Needs autonomy. Likes to work solo or lead.	Likes some independence and some cooperation. Can lead or follow.	Prefers cooperation, teamwork, collaboration, and consensus.

INFORMATION

PRACTICAL	**MIXED**	**VISIONARY**
Detail-oriented. Trusts experience. Prefers precedent over innovation.	Sees big picture and details. Focuses on precedents and possibilities.	Big-picture-oriented. Easily envisions possibilities. Misses details.

OUTLOOK

OPTIMISTIC	**MIXED**	**CAUTIOUS**
Confident of success. Expects good results and overlooks problems.	Realistically evaluates chances of success and likely troubles.	Anticipates trouble. Tries to prevent problems. May aim too low.

DECISION

ANALYTIC	**MIXED**	**EMPATHETIC**
Oriented to facts and data. Objective. Decides by logic.	Makes decisions based on both facts and feelings.	Relationship-oriented. Makes decisions based on feelings.

PLANNING

STRUCTURED	**MIXED**	**FLEXIBLE**
Prefers order, schedules, planning, closure, and few surprises.	Plans while staying open to change. Likes some surprises.	Keeps options open. Avoids planning. Likes choices and surprises.

OUTGOING SOCIAL STYLE

With an Outgoing Social Style, Laura thrives on social contact and likes to spend her days with people. She enjoys multitasking and places full of activity. For example, after taking her children to school, Laura volunteered at their school for several hours before attending a political-action committee meeting or meeting friends for lunch. When tired, she reenergizes by unwinding with people—for instance, by spending time with her two sisters or going to neighborhood gatherings. With her Outgoing style, Laura gains self-insight through talking with others, ideally in a group, and capturing the insight afterward in writing. As you'll see later in the book, Laura's needs for social contact led her to plan a new phase that involves spending her days with people.

CONTEMPLATIVE SOCIAL STYLE

Jeanne, the former community-college instructor with a Contemplative Social Style, needs solitude for reflection during her days and likes to plan her social contacts. Jeanne enjoys time by herself working on her novel in her quiet office. She connects best with people one-to-one, such as reading aloud to her visually impaired neighbor, and interacts most freely with close friends. Reserved with strangers, she attends large gatherings sparingly, because for her they take energy; she reenergizes in solitude.

Jeanne prefers tackling one task at a time without distractions; she doesn't like to multitask, and might let a phone call go to voice mail instead of answering if she's deep in thought. Jeanne, like other Contemplative individuals, gains self-understanding first through solitary reflection and writing. Then she explores and confirms her understanding by talking one-to-one with a close friend—not in a group, like Laura. Jeanne planned for a new phase that includes a mix of quiet solitude and one-to-one social connections that suit her Social Style.

✻   ✻   ✻

You'll learn your Social Style, and how to use that self-knowledge to plan your Next Phase, in chapter 4.

2. What Is Your Stress Style? Responsive vs. Resilient

Your sensitivity to stress and how quickly you recover from setbacks reflect your Stress Style: Responsive, Resilient, or Mixed. Those with Responsive Stress Styles are sensitive to the stress that accompanies changes in life, get upset under pressure or adversity, and need comforting and supportive settings. Those with Resilient Stress Styles stay calm under pressure, recover quickly from setbacks, see demands and changes as enjoyable challenges, and may overextend themselves because they overestimate their capacities to handle stress.

RESPONSIVE STRESS STYLE

Jeanne illustrates a Responsive Stress Style—along with self-awareness and deliberate management of stress. Knowing that she is sensitive to pressure and stress, she has carefully arranged for protective buffers and support systems. She lives on a quiet street. She maintains supportive relationships with people around her, including neighbors and a few close friends on the faculty at the college. She has also learned to expect to react to stress with physical symptoms, like headaches or high blood pressure, so she goes to great lengths to take care of her health. She gets daily exercise by walking where she needs to go. She watches her diet and regularly meditates.

RESILIENT STRESS STYLE

Laura exemplifies the Resilient Stress Style. Calm under pressure and self-composed in dealing with changes and challenges, Laura recovers quickly from setbacks. Her stress-hardy personality enabled her to manage three children and commitments to school and volunteer organizations. Laura sometimes underestimated the demands facing her and overextended herself without realizing it. That's typical of many Resilient individuals—and that's when the stress reaction shows up! Occasionally Laura would push herself too hard even for someone so stress tolerant, and end up in bed with a cold, virus, or flu.

You'll learn your Stress Style in chapter 5.

3. What Is Your Activity Style? Independent vs. Interdependent

Your Activity Style reflects your preference for choosing and directing your own activities—the Independent Activity Style—versus cooperating, collaborating, and meshing your activities with those of others—the Interdependent Activity Style—or a mix. This preference determines how much autonomy and self-direction you want. Those with an Independent style need autonomy and solo activity, and prefer to direct themselves (or direct others) rather than have others influence what they do. Those with Interdependent styles need teamwork in their lives; value cooperation, consensus, and collaboration; and require less autonomy.

In our seminars and classes, someone usually asks, "Isn't your Activity Style determined by your Social Style? If you're Outgoing, won't you prefer Interdependent activities?" The question makes sense, because Social Style and Activity Style do have a lot in common. An Outgoing individual needs social contact, and an Interdependent person needs teamwork; both involve connecting with people. The two preferences do tend to correlate: Outgoing individuals often prefer Interdependent activities.

But not always. Leaders, for example, tend have Outgoing and *Independent* styles—they crave social contact, but they also prefer activities in which they can lead rather than following someone else's directions. As you might expect, those with Contemplative Social Styles also often prefer Independent, self-directed activities.

INDEPENDENT ACTIVITY STYLE

Laura exemplifies the take-charge-of-my-destiny, Independent Activity Style. She prefers to direct her own pursuits. With her Outgoing Social Style, she also needs to connect with other people, where she likes to take the lead. She loved running her household and raising her children, and enjoys leading political committees and volunteer groups. Competitive individual (self-directed) sports might appeal to her, like singles tennis or karate.

For someone with a Contemplative Social Style, Independent activity often means a solitary pursuit, such as doing research, writing, or composing music.

INTERDEPENDENT ACTIVITY STYLE

Jeanne exemplifies the Interdependent Activity Style. She prefers to cooperate with others at both work and play. Jeanne has collaborated closely on her novel for several decades with her coauthor, Lois, reflecting her needs for cooperation and teamwork. She enjoys mentoring younger colleagues (one-to-one, because she has a Contemplative Social Style). She likes to walk with a friend when she can, and enjoys Interdependent volunteer activities: reading aloud to her blind neighbor and teaching English to Spanish-speaking immigrants.

You'll learn your Activity Style in chapter 6.

4. What Is Your Information Style? Practical vs. Visionary

How you approach assimilating and retaining information determines your Information Style. If you have a Practical Information Style, you focus on precedent and specific steps. Practical individuals have difficulty seeing innovative options or future scenarios, and may dislike theories or abstract concepts. Someone who has a Visionary Information Style focuses on the future, the big picture. Visionaries have trouble with concrete steps and details.

PRACTICAL INFORMATION STYLE

Laura, comfortable with tradition, exemplifies a Practical Information Style. She easily mastered the daily demands of running a household and relies on precedent. When she remodeled rooms in her home, she used a tasteful blend of traditional styles and utilitarian, user-friendly arrangements. Laura, like others with her Practical style, had trouble envisioning the future very far ahead. Her "empty next" represented a big challenge.

VISIONARY INFORMATION STYLE

Jeanne, who has a Visionary Information Style, imagines future possibilities. In whatever she does, Jeanne visualizes the big picture in life. As an illustration, when she first heard of the Spanish-speaking immigrants who had moved into her neighborhood, she thought of their need to retain part of their culture yet fully function while living in the United States. When she volunteered to teach English to the newcomers, she saw herself as part of a global effort.

You'll learn your Information Style in chapter 7.

5. What Is Your Outlook Style? Optimistic vs. Cautious

Your Outlook Style comprises the way you evaluate future possibilities, ranging from an Optimistic focus on expected benefits and success to a Cautious emphasis on the risks, problems, and possibilities for failure. A Mixed Outlook style would emphasize both equally.

In evaluating options, a person with an Optimistic Outlook tends to overestimate benefits and underestimate risks. In contrast, the individual with a Cautious Outlook tends to overestimate risks and may dismiss good options too quickly. In setting goals the Optimistic person may aim too high, while the Cautious individual may aim too low. Gaining self-insight into your Outlook Style preference will help you evaluate your options in a realistic way.

OPTIMISTIC OUTLOOK

Laura's Optimistic Outlook Style came across in everything she did. Her glass-half-full-because-I-haven't-started-yet style led her to set high goals at home, for her children, and in her community affiliations. When it came time to follow through, she sometimes found she had badly underestimated the effort required. For example, one political commitment took months longer than she originally expected.

CAUTIOUS OUTLOOK

Attuned to possible difficulties, Jeanne offers an example of a Cautious Outlook. She tends to see the glass as half empty. Jeanne realizes that problems inevitably arise, so she expects things to go wrong and plans ahead to prevent trouble. For example, she bought a health-care plan at a hospital near her house in case she needs medical care on short notice. "You never know; I might break a leg."

You'll learn your Outlook Style in chapter 8.

6. What Is Your Decision Style? Empathetic vs. Analytic

What you emphasize when making a decision—peoples' feelings and personal relationships (heart) or logic and objective analysis of results (head)—reflects your Decision Style. An individual with an Empathetic Decision Style makes decisions based on relationships and loyalties. Someone with an Analytic Decision Style focuses on objective data, costs, and benefits when making decisions. A person with a Mixed style uses a combination of both, and can end up balanced or ambivalent.

EMPATHETIC DECISION STYLE

Those with an Empathetic personality like Jeanne's focus on understanding peoples' feelings and nurturing relationships. Empathetics

"At our age, they say the glass is half full. But which half?"

are sympathetic, considerate, and usually aware of emotional nuance. For example, concerned about her visually impaired neighbor, Jeanne found an opportunity to assist by reading aloud from the newspaper each day. She chose to give to others out of concern for their emotional needs, not because it would make her money.

ANALYTIC DECISION STYLE

Laura exemplifies the Analytic Decision Style. Her ability to focus on the facts and make an objective analysis of results and costs was an asset in her career as a homemaker. Dispassionate and logical,

Laura sometimes tends to overlook feelings where relationships are concerned. For instance, she admits to pushing her children harder in school than they liked at the time, and she expected them to perform regardless of their feelings about the teacher or class.

You'll learn your Decision Style in chapter 9.

What Is Your Preference?

The personality traits in the My Next Phase Profiles represent preferences ranging between two opposing tendencies, such as making decisions using logic versus emotion or seeing the details or the big picture. The two opposites create tension. We resolve the opposing motivations in different ways at different times, so we don't always act consistently. For example, Jeanne, normally a quiet and reserved Contemplative, might act extroverted and gregarious while teaching a class. Likewise, Laura, a talkative woman with an Outgoing style, might listen much more than talk while participating in a seminar.

---

7. What Is Your Planning Style? Flexible vs. Structured

Your Planning Style can range from a preference for spontaneity and open options to a preference for predictability and planning ahead. It could also be Mixed (a blend of the two). Someone with a Flexible Planning Style, like Laura, likes to have choices, and resists planning and commitments as long as possible—maybe too long. In contrast, an individual with a Structured Planning Style, like Jeanne, likes to plan and schedule in advance, and wants an agenda as soon as possible—maybe too soon. Others might have a mixture of both preferences.

FLEXIBLE PLANNING STYLE

Laura, the stay-at-home mom, exemplifies a Flexible Planning Style. She says her motto is *Carpe diem* ("Seize the day"). Spontaneous and comfortable with ambiguity, she enjoys variety and surprises. She liked raising three children and running a household, even if it seemed chaotic at times. She adapted easily to the fluid schedules and shifting demands of her role as a homemaker. Laura doesn't like to plan very much; it takes effort and concentration. She chafes under the constraints of rules, and if she disagrees with the rules themselves will fight to change them, as she did in some of her political activities. Because Laura prefers options, she doesn't like choosing. She might put off planning as long as she possibly can. Laura likes change in her environment, so she enjoys starting new home-decoration projects and often rearranges, refurnishes, and repaints rooms in her home for fun. For Laura, activities that call for rigid, fixed schedules might prove difficult and demanding.

STRUCTURED PLANNING STYLE

Jeanne has a Structured Planning Style and enjoys living in an organized way. If she had a motto, it could be "No surprises." Jeanne methodically plotted many things in her life, from the classes she taught, to her phased retirement from teaching, to paying off her home mortgage with her early retirement pay. She likes having a routine: writing in the mornings, walking to her appointments in the afternoons (for exercise as well as transportation), teaching her English classes for Spanish-speaking immigrants. Generally striving to stay organized and orderly, Jeanne wants things settled and scheduled. Comfortable with rules, she enjoys predictability—and doesn't like surprises or unexpected changes of plan. For Jeanne, activities that call for dealing often with unexpected changes might prove difficult and demanding.

Jeanne's Personality Profile

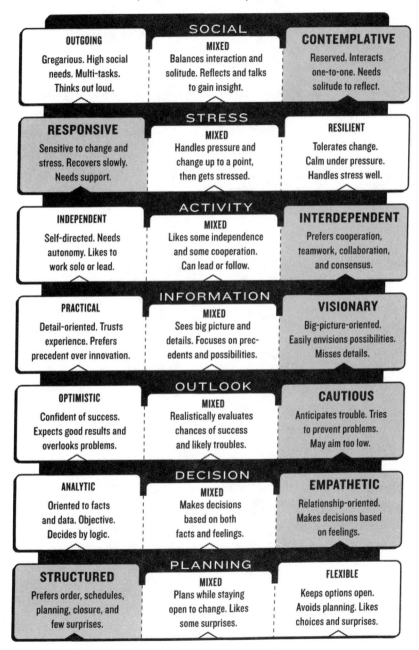

You'll learn your Planning Style in chapter 10.

DISCOVER YOUR PERSONALITY PROFILE

Are the pieces of the personality puzzle beginning to fit together? Perhaps you see yourself having some of the same personality traits as Jeanne or Laura. Maybe you can recognize similar traits in family members, friends, or coworkers. Now that you have a new awareness about personality, please move on to chapter 4 and begin to identify your seven traits and build your own Personality Profile.

PART II

The Seven Personality Traits That Determine Your Best Retirement

CHAPTER 4

What Is Your Social Style?

How Understanding Your Social Style Will
Keep You From "Flunking" Retirement

HOUSEBOUND AND UNHAPPY

Mark has a gift for remembering faces. If he has met you even once, he'll greet you by name. Gregarious and persuasive, Mark is the quintessential "people person"—his quick wit and ready sense of humor make him ideally suited to his job in sales and marketing.

For his entire career, Mark spent his days going from meeting to meeting, group to group. Often the center of a gathering, he enjoyed working with clients all day and unwinding with his wife, Eva, in the evening at a dinner party. Mark thrives on social contact and draws energy from people.

You can imagine our surprise when Mark announced that he had bought a lakeside property in an isolated, mountainous area of Wyoming on which he and Eva would build their retirement dream home. Mark decided he would leave his sales career at its peak. "I'm ready for a change," he said.

"Won't you miss all your friends from work, all your contacts in the city?" we asked.

"Maybe at first," Mark replied. He assured us that he'd stay in touch by phone. He loved the serenity of his new lake place; it seemed like paradise to him.

Mark and Eva settled into their new retirement home in the fall and enjoyed the first part of retirement. But for someone as outgoing and gregarious as Mark, spending any length of time in a quiet and out-of-the-way retreat—even a dream home—soon brings feelings of isolation and even depression. When a few months of freezing winter temperatures left Mark snowed in and homebound, our friend became discontented and unhappy.

It's not easy to admit making a bad decision, especially when it involves both a large purchase and a relocation. As we predicted, though, after living away from his energizing workplace and his co-workers, friends, and clients for a few months, our Outgoing friend realized that he had failed at retirement—Mark underestimated how much he needed people around him to stay happy.

LOIS'S CLOSE CALL

After a career starting as a data-entry clerk and taking evening classes to qualify for her position as senior programmer at an information systems company, Lois, sixty, decided to try something new in her life. Tired of living alone in the cold Northeast, she considered buying a small unit in a popular retirement community on Florida's east coast that specialized in directed social activities.

"I read the colorful brochures and even watched the video they sent," Lois said. "While it did seem quite busy, I thought it might work for my retirement. The warm temperatures appealed to me, and I enjoy swimming for exercise."

Then about a week before the large deposit was due, a colleague suggested that Lois take the personality inventory at www.MyNext Phase.com to make sure she was suited to a social retirement filled with people, parties, and planned activities. Lois soon learned that she had a Contemplative, or introverted, personality—well suited

Oh, nothing . . . it's just a hot flash.

to the job she had prepared to leave, but much less compatible with the sociable recreational community in Florida where she had planned to move.

Lois ultimately decided that moving to a community focused on social events made no sense for someone with her personality. Lois's current job called for her to master new skills and work on creative solo projects. She just didn't want to give this up. Instead of moving, she decided to save her money, keep her job a few more years, and look for a better fit. Maybe she could downshift to part-time consulting for her company's warmer Georgia office?

What makes the difference between success and failure in retirement? We've found that those who succeed make a point of understanding themselves, and they plan for futures compatible with their personalities. Those who fail tend to go ahead with plans that don't suit them—reflecting a lack of *self-awareness*.

WHY SUCCESS IN RETIREMENT REQUIRES SELF-UNDERSTANDING

Lois gained self-understanding after taking the personality test at www.MyNextPhase.com. Realizing that she had a Contemplative Social Style, she decided against moving to a sociable retirement community. Luckily, she hadn't mailed her deposit or quit her full-time job!

In contrast, Mark had grown unaware of just how much social contact his Outgoing personality needed, and how much energy he drew from interacting with the people around him. He'd planned to retire to a remote location where he really couldn't expect enough personal contact with other people to meet his social needs. As predicted, the environment soon proved incompatible with his personality.

Are you ready to understand your Social Style—Outgoing or Contemplative? Go ahead and take the first personality test on page 60. It may confirm what you already know, or help you learn something new about yourself.

SELF-UNDERSTANDING FOR YOUR NEXT PHASE

In the beginning of the chapter, we talked about Lois, who succeeded at her Next Phase, and Mark, who outright failed. What made the difference between success and failure? Lois succeeded because she took time for self-understanding. She learned more about her personality, particularly her Social Style (Contemplative), and then made a plan for her future—staying at her full-time job—compatible with her personality. Mark, like many retirees, failed by making plans that didn't suit his personality (Outgoing)—reflecting a lack of self-awareness. We hope he'll rethink his future.

Remember Ron, the production manager in chapter 1? He underestimated his needs for face time with people when he retired to play golf. At work Ron interacted with people all day, which suited his Outgoing personality. He didn't realize how much social contact he needed, and overestimated how much time he would have with Jill and his few friendships outside work, who had lives of their own!

If Ron had reviewed a typical workweek, he'd have seen that for twenty years he spent five days a week in practically constant, face-to-face interaction. Trying to replace that with golf outings would be difficult at best! His wife, Jill, saw that right away and told her sister, "I know Ron better than he knows himself. He'll be bored within weeks."

As Jill predicted, Ron did get bored. He missed his friends from work, and later realized how much. What about you? Will you fail at retirement on your first try? Or do you have the self-understanding you need to avoid a mistake like Mark's or Ron's?

WRITING WITH THE OPPOSITE HAND

You'll need a pen or pencil and a blank sheet of paper for this next exercise. Using your preferred hand, write your full name in the middle of the sheet of paper. Now transfer the pen or pencil into your other (nonpreferred) hand and write your name again directly underneath.

Compare the two efforts. If you are ambidextrous and can write with both hands (few can), the two efforts may look alike. But if you're like us—and most people—your second effort probably looks shaky and uneven, and maybe even stops in the middle.

What does writing with the opposite hand have to do with personality? Plenty! Think of your Social Style as being either right- or left-handed. If you're Outgoing like Mark, you naturally enjoy talking with people throughout your day, while having to spend a day alone can be torture. But if Outgoing individuals move to remote spots for retirement (like Mark did) without the stimulation of face time with other people, they find themselves in settings

PERSONALITY QUIZ #1: WHAT IS YOUR SOCIAL STYLE? OUTGOING VS. CONTEMPLATIVE

Consider how you think, feel, and act *most of the time* when away from work and free to be yourself. Mark each statement *true* or *false*. If a statement is sometimes true and other times false, mark it *true* if it describes you even *slightly* more often than not. Avoid responses based on your work role or what others expect or how you'd like to be. If in doubt, go with your *first reaction* or *intuition*.

True	*False*	
❑	❑	1. I enjoy parties and social gatherings, and I find them energizing.
❑	❑	2. After working with people all day, I recharge by unwinding with friends.
❑	❑	3. I work best in a busy place full of activity.
❑	❑	4. I clarify my ideas and feelings by talking about them with others.
❑	❑	5. I'm often one of the last people to leave a social gathering.
❑	❑	6. I form relationships quickly and easily.
❑	❑	7. My working environment usually bustles with people and activity.
❑	❑	8. I enjoy mixing and mingling at a social gathering.
❑	❑	9. I have a wide circle of friends and acquaintances.
❑	❑	10. I get my best ideas and insights from talking with people.

_____ My total score (count the number of boxes marked *true*)

What Your Score Means

A score of 7, 8 , 9, or 10 indicates an Outgoing style—the higher the score, the more consistent your preference for this style. *A score of 4, 5, or 6 indicates a Mixed Outgoing/Contemplative style. A score of 0, 1, 2, or 3 shows a Contemplative Social Style*—the lower the score, the more consistent your preference.

Outgoing Social Style (7–10): You draw energy from people and your environment. You like being with people and enjoy companionship. Usually you have several projects going at once. Outgoing, gregarious, and extroverted, you enjoy social activities and gatherings. Being alone can be tiring; you reenergize by spending time with people.

Mixed Contemplative/Outgoing Social Style (4–6): You gain energy from both people and solitude, though after very much time with either you tend to want the other. Equally comfortable with reflection and action, you strive to balance inward- and outward-oriented sides of your personality, and find it draining to dwell too long with either side. You solve problems and make decisions by thinking them through by yourself and talking them through with others. Usually at ease by yourself or in a group, you gravitate toward small-group activities with a few friends or acquaintances. While you can concentrate on one thing for a while, you enjoy varying your activities and occasionally working on several things at once.

Contemplative Social Style (1–3): You tend to draw energy from solitary reflection and prefer to focus on one thing at a time, in a quiet setting without distraction. Inward-oriented, reserved, and introverted, you usually prefer one-to-one conversations and occasional small-group activities. Social gatherings can be tiring; you reenergize by spending time alone.

Your Personality Profile

Now that you have the results from your first Personality Quiz, you can start building your Personality Profile. Eventually your profile will have results for all seven traits, like the examples of profiles in the previous chapter for Jeanne and Laura. For now you have results on the first trait, one of seven in your profile. Record your Social Style (Contemplative, Mixed, or Outgoing) on your first Personality Profile module below. (You might use a highlighter for this.) Then turn to the last chapter in the book (page 185), where you'll find the same image as part of your blank Personality Profile showing all seven traits. Record your first result there, too. After each quiz you can add another result. When you've finished all seven, you'll be ready to review the profile where it is in the last chapter, on your way to planning your Next Phase.

My Social Style

OUTGOING	SOCIAL MIXED	CONTEMPLATIVE
Gregarious. High social needs. Multi-tasks. Thinks out loud.	Balances interaction and solitude. Reflects and talks to gain insight.	Reserved. Interacts one-to-one. Needs solitude to reflect.

outside their zones of comfort that require tremendous energy just to adapt—like *writing with the opposite hand*. It makes life—and retirement—uncomfortable, like writing your name the second time in this exercise.

ADAPTING YOUR SOCIAL STYLE TO YOUR LIFE

Do you remember how you acted when you were a teenager? Maybe you were exuberant and extroverted and attracted many friends. Or maybe you were quiet and introverted, avoiding the center of attention. As teenagers we acted out our personality traits most consistently across situations. If you were Outgoing as a teenager, that's probably your preference today. The same is true if you scored Contemplative or Mixed.

With age we become less stereotypical as we adapt to work and other environments. For example, if you have an Outgoing Social Style, you may act calmer and more thoughtful than you did as a gregarious adolescent. Learned adaptations temper our tendencies to act out our preferences. Yet under stress we may revert quickly, almost reflexively, to our preferences.

Now if you overemphasize one of two opposite traits, such as Outgoing or Contemplative, and never learn to do the other, you resemble the carpenter with just one tool in his toolbox, a hammer. If your only solution is a hammer, you treat all problems as nails. A hammer has many apt uses, like opening coconuts and taking out dents in fenders. But try using it to remove a splinter in your thumb! Even people who have a strong preference for one of two opposite traits eventually learn the skills of the other. Or in other words, we *adapt* as we mature. You may prefer one of the two traits in each pair (your personality) but still acquire the skills of the opposite. This is called adaptation.

Adaptation takes effort and concentration, like learning to write with the opposite hand. It grows easier over time, and eventually you can get proficient. You'll discover ways to manage the tasks you find difficult. Even so, adapting can take hard work, especially at first. If you find the results rewarding, you may continue long enough to develop a valuable lifelong skill—as Jeanne, the former college English instructor, discovered after she conquered her anxiety about public speaking.

"I used to be shy as a teenager," said Jeanne. "But that changed when I got my first job. After I finished my second degree in English, I knew I couldn't earn a living as a young writer. So I really only had one other choice: go into teaching—even though I dreaded the idea of speaking in front of groups."

Jeanne realized she would have to adapt. "It took all my strength to give those first few lectures to classrooms full of college students nearly my age. I felt drained!"

She quickly found she needed time alone afterward to recharge. "Without that quiet time I was exhausted all day. For years, the running joke in the faculty lounge was that you could always find Jeanne in a far nook at the library for an hour after teaching a class."

Forty years after mastering the difficult (for her) skill of public speaking, Jeanne left her job as English instructor. She left the classroom—and her reason for adapting.

You may wonder what happens at retirement—if you choose to leave the workplace and you no longer have to adapt. Do you keep doing what you learned to do at work?

If you're aware of how you've adapted, you can deliberately choose how you'll carry those learned habits into your new phase. As for Jeanne, she decided to continue with learned habits. "After forty years, I think I've gotten pretty good at classroom teaching. And I still enjoy it—in moderation. I still need my time alone to recharge afterward. But I know how to manage that. That's why I decided to make classroom teaching part of my retirement."

Unlike Jeanne, Laura chose *not* to continue her adaptation. "For years, I learned to adapt in order to do the household chores. I cannot stand doing solitary chores! After cleaning bathrooms and mopping, I'd always reward myself and meet some friends for lunch or shopping. Now with the kids gone, I'm going to reward myself and hire a housekeeper. No more chores for me! I'm moving forward with my life and focusing on what I really enjoy."

What about you? How have you adapted your Social Style to your workplace? To answer, you have to be aware of your Social Style (Outgoing, Contemplative, or Mixed), and remember what you did to adjust it to your work (and probably still do if you think about it).

Unfortunately, it's all too easy to forget how you've adapted after several decades, as habits become ingrained and drop out of awareness. As an example, consider how automatically you drive your car. How many times have you gotten in your car, buckled your seat belt, and driven to the grocery store without even thinking about driving? What about giving speeches to large groups?

As you continue to read this book, think about how you've adapted your personality to your work. Also, consider the skills you've had to work most diligently to develop in your career, especially if they were the opposite of your personality trait. Use the Personality Quiz and exercises in this chapter—and in the upcoming chapters—to understand yourself. With a foundation of self-awareness, you can plan your Next Phase with your Personality Profile in mind and create your best retirement on the first try.

As you continue on to chapter 5—What Is Your Stress Style?— you'll gauge the changes in your life and learn about the stress you can expect from those changes. The next Personality Quiz will help you identify your Stress Style, how your personality deals with the stress accompanying life change, and what this means for your Next Phase.

CHAPTER 5

What Is Your Stress Style?

How Understanding Your Stress Style Will
Make Your Transition Easier

TOM'S UNEXPECTED NEW PHASE

Tom, fifty-six, a computer programmer at an information technology firm, began his bumpy journey to a new phase abruptly, with an unexpected layoff. "It was a rainy Friday morning in February. I went to the office early so I could wrap up some work before the weekend. When I opened my e-mail, I found a message ordering me to a meeting at nine a.m. with my manager and the HR representative."

Tom continued, "The rest of the day is a complete blur. I joined maybe twenty other employees in a conference room. Someone from corporate explained that the company eliminated our jobs to cut costs. After handing out a form letter about the severance package, the HR rep said to clean out our desks, box up our stuff, and leave the building by noon."

Tom's mood changed over the next few days. First he went from shock to disbelief and denial, but that didn't last long. Late Saturday night he had a few drinks too many as he ruminated about the layoff, and anger gave way to depression. Sunday afternoon, when he finally got out of bed, he brooded and wouldn't talk with anyone. He stayed in bed most of Monday, too. Finally that evening he broke his silence.

"Why didn't I see it coming?" Tom said to his wife, Jane. "I guess I should've noticed red flags, but I had no warning. Some people who got laid off from the other department said they'd heard layoffs were coming months earlier. But no one told me about it until after it happened. My manager owed me at least a heads-up. I could've started looking for something else if only I'd known."

The more Tom thought about it, the more he dwelled on the injustices and insults. He couldn't seem to focus for long on his career or his options for the future without lapsing into worry about where the next paycheck would come from. He also fretted how he would cover the tuition payments for his son's first year of college. Completely immobilized, Tom began having trouble sleeping. He knew the severance pay would tide them over for a few months, but Tom saw himself in a race against time to find work before the money ran out—and it looked like he would lose.

By April Tom had sent dozens of e-mails and letters, and interviewed for two positions. He didn't get an offer from either one. Then, while watching the late news one evening, wondering how he'd ever find work and recover financially, Tom felt his heart racing. The next morning he awoke before sunrise, convinced that he was having a heart attack, and worried sick about the cost of a trip to the ER. Jane helped him to calm down and remember he still had a few weeks of company health insurance. Later that morning after a series of tests, the ER doctor said Tom didn't have heart problems, but a severe case of anxiety. He gave Tom some prescription medications and a card with the name and private phone number of a counselor nearby.

Feeling overwhelmed and displaced, Tom saw no choice but to urge Jane to find a job. "You can't depend on me to support us anymore. We need two incomes to recover from this layoff. Otherwise, we'll have to put the house up for sale."

Jane suggested that they rent out the house as a temporary

solution, and move into an inexpensive apartment, to save money. "At least that way we can cover most of the mortgage payments while the two of us look for work." Tom unhappily agreed. Within three weeks they had rented the family home and moved into a one-bedroom apartment on the other side of town, miles away from lifelong friends and neighbors. A few visits to the counselor helped Tom deal with the added stress of losing not only his job, but also his home and his status as family breadwinner.

Major unwanted changes, like those in Tom's life, inevitably create stress. Multiple changes—such as suddenly losing a job, moving to a new home, and becoming a two-job couple (if only one mate worked previously)—combine to create even more stress. Welcome changes, like having a child go away to college, can also add stress, because they call for adjustments. And, unfortunately for Tom, some individuals have particular difficulty dealing with stress from life's demands. With his stress-sensitive (Responsive) personality, Tom reacted more intensely to his layoff—and had greater difficulty coping with it—than his coworkers.

Whatever life brings, your personality drives the way you perceive life change, how much stress you experience from it, and how you cope and adapt. For individuals like Tom, several major life changes all at once can shake the ground underfoot. While his stress-resistant (Resilient) coworkers felt the layoff as a tremor, Tom felt a shock like an earthquake registering more than six points on his personal Richter scale of stress.

After a while, with support from those around him, especially his wife, Tom adjusted. He came to grips with the reality of his new situation and began to contemplate what he'd do next. With help from his counselor, Tom recovered his equilibrium over time and looked ahead to a new phase.

"I outlived everybody on the obituary page today."

KATE WEATHERS THE STORM

Whereas the unexpected layoff hit Tom like a bolt from the blue, Kate, fifty-seven, received word of her impending layoff calmly when her outgoing friend and coworker, Marilyn, brought the news.

"I took some paperwork to Human Resources this morning and walked past the small conference room," Marilyn said in a hushed voice. "You won't like what I heard. Some of our managers were talking about budget cuts, and one of them said layoffs looked inevitable. I heard 'Graphic Arts Department' before someone shut the door."

"Graphic Arts?" Kate asked. "Well, it looks like our days here are numbered. I've looked for work before; I can look again."

Kate had worked as a graphic artist for the same design firm almost twenty years. Her quiet corner office overlooked a lush nature reserve and seemed more like a second home. Many times she worked late because the secluded environment allowed her to concentrate without distraction. Like Tom, Kate has a Contemplative Social Style. However, unlike Tom, who usually stayed to himself, Kate got the latest office news most days from her outgoing friend, Marilyn, so she stayed informed about company politics.

But layoffs? Kate wouldn't wait around doing nothing while the managers decided she was expendable. After all, with her divorce final last month, she had to pay the bills—for herself and her two college-age children.

A week later, after packing a last load of household goods with her art supplies and laptop into her minivan, Kate walked into her Realtor's office and signed the paperwork to start the sale of her house. Now single and living alone, she didn't need the space, and had considered moving since her second child had left for college. She was pleasantly surprised how much the house had gained in value.

"Thanks for the heads-up on the impending job cuts," she told Marilyn the next day. "To get ready, I've decided to sell my house and move in with my parents. They're both elderly and can use my help. Last year they offered me their extra bedroom, so the timing is right. I figure I can use some of the profit from my house to cover my share of the kids' college tuition—and of course pay the bills when the company puts us out on the street. I'll buy some time to plan my next step—look for another job or go freelance with my graphic art. It'll be interesting to see how this unfolds."

Kate faced a stressful transition. Yet she never felt anxious or overwhelmed. Her stress-tolerant personality left her confident that she would weather the storm in her life.

LIFE CHANGE AND STRESS

Tom's layoff and Kate's move to get ready for hers represented major changes in their lives—like the changes that face many baby boomers nearing retirement. Whether you leave a job by choice or involuntarily, retirement brings major life changes and emotional stress.

We all know the standard definition of "stress"—the demands and pressures that each of us experiences each day. These include minor hassles, like traffic jams while driving, or more troubling challenges, like layoff notices, relationship difficulties, or illnesses. The stress response has two parts:

1. Our *perception* of the challenge
2. The automatic physiological reaction called the *"fight-or-flight" response*

We inherited the physiological response from our prehistoric ancestors; it gave them the energy to flee from danger—as it does for us. For instance, stress begins with the perception of trouble, especially if it is alarming enough to represent a threat—such as a charging dog. Fear brings a surge of adrenaline, which sets off the body's preparation to either fight or flee. If you don't regard the dog as a threat, of course, you don't experience this physiological response.

Because stress depends on *perception*, individual reactions vary. For instance, Kate received the news of her coming layoff with relative calm, whereas Tom went into a full-blown fight-or-flight response. His sympathetic nervous system prompted the release of stress hormones such as cortisol. The stress hormones boost blood glucose (sugar) and triglycerides (blood fats) to fuel the fight-or-flight response; thus, you experience a racing heart, fast breathing, and nervous energy.

When the fuel for fighting and running isn't used for those activities, chronic stress leads to health problems such as premature coronary artery disease and heart attack, loss of short-term memory, suppression of the immune system, digestion disorders, and increased muscle tension (aches and pains). Physical exercise tops

PERSONALITY QUIZ #2: WHAT IS YOUR STRESS STYLE? RESPONSIVE VS. RESILIENT

Consider how you think, feel, and act *most of the time* when away from work and free to be yourself. Mark each statement *true* or *false*. If a statement is sometimes true and other times false, mark it *true* if it descirbes you even *slightly* more often than not. Avoid responses based on your work role or what others expect or how you'd like to be. If in doubt, go with your *first reaction* or *intuition*.

True   False

❑   ❑   1. I get upset more easily than I like to admit.

❑   ❑   2. Once upset, I find it takes me a long time to pull myself together.

❑   ❑   3. At times I feel emotionally overwhelmed.

❑   ❑   4. I need to learn better ways to handle stress.

❑   ❑   5. My friends think of me as easily upset.

❑   ❑   6. I tend to get depressed or anxious about future events.

❑   ❑   7. When feeling upset I have a hard time not showing it.

❑   ❑   8. I often feel apprehensive.

❑   ❑   9. Often I wish life didn't have so many pressures and demands.

❑   ❑   10. I wonder how other people manage to remain so calm.

_____   My total score (count the number of boxes marked *true*)

What Your Score Means

A score of 7, 8, 9, or 10 indicates a Responsive Stress Style—the higher the score, the more consistent your preference for a Responsive style. A score of 4, 5, or 6 indicates a Mixed Responsive/Resilient Stress Style. A score of 0, 1, 2, or 3 shows a Resilient Stress Style—the lower the score, the more consistent your preference for a Resilient style.

Responsive Stress Style (7–10): Your sensitivity to changes in your life tends to consume energy and can throw you off balance. Even exciting, attractive new experiences may seem demanding and make you tired, fearful, or anxious. You often prefer to avoid too much challenge, and tend to find change and pressure more upsetting than exciting. You generally cannot easily put disappointments, unwelcome surprises, and setbacks behind you. This process can take some time before you can move on to the next challenge. For a smooth and satisfying retirement, you may need to find ways to handle the transition in small, manageable bites. Possibly, you will need some extra sources of emotional support to help you make the transition to your Next Phase.

Mixed Responsive/Resilient Style (4–6): Sometimes you react strongly to the demands and pressures of life. At other times, you remain calm and composed, depending on the circumstances. When you do become upset, you may quickly bounce back from minor setbacks. However, it takes you much longer to recover your emotional equilibrium after major disturbances. Sometimes you can calm yourself, but when you are very upset, you may rely on others for support. You may notice that you can handle demands and pressures calmly until you reach your personal threshold for overload. Any challenge beyond that threshold might bring an intense response—an apparent overreaction as you switch from Resilient mode to Responsive mode.

Resilient Stress Style (0–3): Your hardy, calm style enables you to manage the transition to retirement with apparent ease. Your resilience allows you to take advantage of opportunities that others might find too emotionally demanding. In transition you'll probably experience less stress and turmoil than your peers. You may even have difficulty empathizing with those who find change and pressure upsetting while you experience them as exciting challenges. Because you cope so well with stress and pressure, you may lose sight of your own limitations. You can expect to get overextended unless you make a conscious effort to manage your commitments.

Your Personality Profile

Record your Stress Style (Responsive, Mixed, or Resilient) on the Personality Profile module below. Then turn to the last chapter in the book (page 185), where you'll find your Personality Profile showing all seven traits. Record the result for your Stress Style there, too, to review before you complete the plan for your Next Phase.

My Stress Style

STRESS		
RESPONSIVE	**MIXED**	**RESILIENT**
Sensitive to change and stress. Recovers slowly. Needs support.	Handles pressure and change up to a point, then gets stressed.	Tolerates change. Calm under pressure. Handles stress well.

the list of preferred methods of managing stress, another reason we include it as one of the five keys to a successful retirement.

EVEN DESIRABLE CHANGES BRING STRESS

In the 1960s psychologists were surprised to learn that desirable changes in life produce stress, including getting married, having a baby, or reaching a personal achievement. Researchers Thomas Holmes and Richard Rahe at the University of Washington quantified the average stress produced by each of forty-three different life events. On their scale from zero to one hundred points, "death of a spouse" rated most stressful at one hundred. They identified getting married (fifty points on their scale) as slightly more stressful than getting fired (forty-seven points). Retirement (forty-five points) ranked tenth on their list of stressful life events.

Research later confirmed that many of the life events near the top of Holmes and Rahe's list, such as getting fired, do create stress. For instance, one study found that an involuntary layoff in the years immediately preceding retirement, as Tom experienced, correlated with decreased physical and emotional health. Another study—at Yale University among people over fifty who lost their jobs—found the risks of stroke and heart attack doubled compared with others of the same age still working.

Psychologists tried for a few years after that to quantify the stress from specific life events—such as retirement. Many eventually gave up on that idea, though, because stress from any one kind of life change varies so much from person to person. So Holmes and Rahe suggested another hypothesis: *the more changes that occur at once, the greater the overall stress*—as stress accumulates with each added change. Research has since confirmed that multiple life changes bring increased stress. The more changes you experience together, the more stress you can expect. Along with getting fired, Tom experienced four other changes on the list of stressful life events. He had a change in finances and in residences. He asked

Symptoms of Stress
Anger
Anxiety
Apathy
Back pain
Colitis
Depression
Fatigue
Headaches
Heart palpitations
Hives
Impotence
Insomnia
Irregular menstrual periods
Irritability
Irritable bowel syndrome (IBS)
Lack of sexual desire
Mood swings
Neck pain
Rapid pulse
Rashes
Short-term memory loss
Weight gain or loss

Desirable Life Changes That Bring Stress
Building a new home
Child going away to college
Getting a promotion at work
New family member, like a grandchild
Starting a new business
Traveling
Winning a lottery

his wife to find work, and his son recently left home for college. He experienced five stressful life events, counting the layoff, all in a few months. No wonder he had trouble sleeping (a sixth change)!

Retirement can represent an especially stressful event, because it involves so many changes all at once. For example, when Jack left his job as a chemist to move to Myrtle Beach (page 20), he lost his regular paycheck and began drawing income from savings (a financial change). He changed residences and moved away from neighbors and friends. He also began spending much more time with his wife, a change in their marriage. However, Jack made the adjustment to a new life at Myrtle Beach with no apparent signs of stress. He also deliberately chose to retire. Research confirms that change voluntarily chosen, like Jack's retirement, brings much less stress than when the same change comes involuntarily.

Yet Tom and Kate both faced involuntary changes in their lives and reacted very differently. Why? How would you or someone in your family react to an involuntary layoff? The answer lies in personality traits, specifically, Stress Style (Responsive, Mixed, or Resilient; see Personality Quiz #2 on page 72).

Undesirable Life Changes That Bring Stress

Cancellation of health insurance
Death of family member
Diagnosis of life-threatening disease
Getting fired from a job
Loss of income
Marital problems
Moving away from family and friends
Serious injury requiring hospitalization

CAN YOU CHANGE YOUR STRESS STYLE?
(. . . *PROBABLY NOT*)

Juanita, fifty-two, told us she scored as highly Responsive and asked how she could change her Stress Style. "Any stress in my life makes me feel like the earth is caving in. I want to toughen up and be Resilient like my husband."

We have heard this plea from others who scored as Responsive, like Juanita. Like it or not, you probably can't change your Stress Style—Responsive, Mixed, or Resilient. It is pretty much wired in: you are who you are! If you have a Responsive Style, you'll tend to experience more symptoms of stress, and for longer, than your hardier friends. However, you can learn ways of managing stress and avoid many of the symptoms. For instance, we introduced Juanita to *relaxation training*. It helped her, as it has helped many, to cope with stress. Others successfully use *meditation* to manage stress. We ourselves rely on the workhorse of stress management: daily *physical exercise*. Whether you are Responsive or Resilient, all of these techniques can help you to manage stress.

Maybe you saw Steven Spielberg's movie *Jurassic Park*, in which visitors to a remote jungle island see living dinosaurs. In one memorable scene, the driver of a Jeep looks in his rearview mirror and sees a *Tyrannosaurus rex*. It appears small above the printed message, "*Objects in the mirror may be closer than they appear.*" The riders in the Jeep turn around, and through the rear window they see what the movie audience already sees: the huge, toothy *Tyrannosaurus rex* looming above the fleeing Jeep. Another quick glance in the rearview mirror shows the monstrous dinosaur far away, the size of a lizard.

If You Have a Resilient Stress Style—You See Problems in a Jurassic Park Rearview Mirror

Those with a Resilient Stress Style perceive life's demands as small and manageable, like a dinosaur shrunk to lizard size in the Jurassic Park rearview mirror. Those with Resilient Stress Styles feel not only confident that they can handle life's problems, they may also regard the problems as interesting challenges to overcome. Research confirms that those with confidence in their abilities to manage stress actually experience fewer symptoms of stress than others do. Indeed, if you have a Resilient style, you may seek challenges in your life and might even grow bored if you don't have something worthy to contend with.

If You Have a Responsive Stress Style—You See Problems in a Magnifying Mirror

Responsive personalities see with magnifying mirrors that make lizards look like dinosaurs. Because life's stressors appear much bigger than they really are, any life change can overwhelm the more sensitive, Responsive individuals.

If You Have a Mixed Stress Style—You See Problems in an Accurate or Shifty Mirror

If you have a Mixed Responsive/Resilient Stress Style, you may tend to see life's challenges in a mirror that neither magnifies nor shrinks them, but accurately reflects their size. Or you may have another, common experience: a stress threshold and a shifty mirror. As long as you don't face too many challenges at once, they'll seem manageable, and you'll see them in a Jurassic Park monster-shrinking mirror. When you get one more pressure than you can handle, your mirror might switch to magnifying mode and you'll suddenly feel overwhelmed. One small demand can put you over the tipping point, from Resilient mode to Responsive mode. If you have a Mixed Stress Style, look back over the times you've experienced stress. You might notice a threshold. Up to a point, you're okay (Resilient within limits), and beyond that point—maybe only a tiny bit beyond it—you fall apart (Responsive if over threshold). If so, you'd better learn where your threshold is.

HOW MUCH CHANGE ARE YOU DEALING WITH?

In talking with people considering retirement, we've heard about a wide variety of experiences. People describe situations that range from practically no change at all to a few changes in otherwise stable circumstances to major transitions that involve changes in nearly all facets of life. Sometimes they don't realize how much is changing in their lives. To help people quickly gauge how much change they face, we devised a short questionnaire.

Our Life-Change Inventory lists twelve Life Domains. By noting whether you face major change in each one, then counting the number of domains undergoing change, you can compute your Life-Change Index (see below). It gives you a sense of how much change you face. Knowing your Stress Style, you can prepare to deal with the changes.

Compute Your Life-Change Index

Your Life-Change Index indicates the overall amount of change in your life, much like the Richter scale measures the overall impact of an earthquake. It comes from the brief questionnaire opposite.

Your Life-Change Index

Count the number of boxes you checked. That is your Life-Change Index.

What It Means

LIFE-CHANGE INDEX—0, 1, OR 2

Your personal Stress Style determines how you respond to life change. If your Life-Change Index is 0, 1, or 2, and you have a Resilient style, you probably won't notice much. If you have a Responsive style, the changes probably won't seem too difficult to manage. While you may experience some stress, it probably will not be very intense.

LIFE-CHANGE INVENTORY

For each of the twelve Life Domains listed here, check the box if you experienced a major change in the past year, or if you expect a major change in the coming year. If you have experienced no change or only minor change in one of the domains, leave the box blank. If you are unsure whether a change is *major,* it probably isn't.

Life Domain	Major change? (Check if yes)
1. **Mate**—Relationship with spouse or life partner	❏
2. **Work**—Paid job, profession, occupation, business, or calling	❏
3. **Health**—Wellness, fitness, eating, sleeping, personal care	❏
4. **Family**—Children, parents, siblings, relatives	❏
5. **Self-development**—Education, training, workshops, self-study	❏
6. **Money**—Finances, income, bills, credit, loans, taxes	❏
7. **Friends**—Your personal and social connections, near and far	❏
8. **Service**—Volunteer or pro bono work, assistance to others, giving	❏
9. **Home**—Location, design, furnishing, upkeep, routine maintenance	❏
10. **Recreation**—Fun, leisure, play, hobbies, travel, recreation	❏
11. **Spirituality**—Church, religion, introspection	❏
12. **Community**—Involvement in governance, civic organizations, clubs	❏

My Life Change Index (# of boxes checked) _____

LIFE-CHANGE INDEX—3 OR 4

If your Life-Change Index is 3 or 4, and you have a Resilient Stress Style, you can expect the changes to prove somewhat challenging—difficult enough to require attention, but manageable. With a Mixed Stress Style, you could approach your stress threshold. If you have a Responsive style, changes in three or four life domains will likely prove stressful and difficult, possibly extremely upsetting, perhaps overwhelming and debilitating.

LIFE-CHANGE INDEX—5 OR HIGHER

If your Life-Change Index reaches 5 or higher, you face enough change in your life to require serious, sustained attention. If you have a Resilient Stress Style, you can manage the changes without too much strain, though you'll certainly notice the effort. If you have a Mixed style you'll notice the stress and at times you'll probably feel the strain, or want some support, or both. If you have a Responsive style, you'll find the changes very upsetting or worse, and you'll probably need sustained support from those close to you.

When we gave one of our first seminars in 1999, we asked the attendees to complete an early version of the Life-Change Inventory and check the life domains in which they experienced change. After a while we asked how many domains people had checked. A middle-aged woman, Susanna, stood up and said she had checked eight life domains. "I wondered why I felt so disoriented and overloaded," she exclaimed. "I had no idea my life was changing so much!"

Susanna went through her list. She had enough changes in her life to make anyone's head spin, even the most Resilient! Not only was she finishing her divorce and her master's degree, but she was relocating to a another state, purchasing a new condominium, starting a new job in a different field, and saying good-bye to her last child leaving for college.

Susanna's Life-Change Index = 8

1. **Mate:** Recently divorced
2. **Work:** New job in a different field
3. **Family:** Second (and last) child left home for college
4. **Self-development:** Finishing a master's degree
5. **Friends:** Relocating away from her lifelong friends and some family members
6. **Home:** New condo in another state
7. **Recreation:** Looking for affordable health club or fitness center near her condo
8. **Spirituality:** Looking for a synagogue near her new condo

At the time we were surprised that Susanna was unaware how much her life was changing. How could she not know such a thing? We realized that she must have an unusual tolerance for stress. Even so, she must have had a hard time coping. Susanna confirmed that she did feel overwhelmed. Later on we understood why she was unaware of her circumstances. Stress produces what psychologists call narrowing of attention—focusing just on the most urgent details and overlooking all else. (Think of the last time you tried to drive and talk on your cell phone at the same time.) Because we have limited cognitive capacity, we can hold only so much in mind. We focus only on what matters most. Susanna had become so preoccupied with day-to-day responsibilities that she had no mental capacity left over. Her situation reinforced the importance of taking time to assess the situation.

Consider Tom and Kate. Here are the life changes they experienced, in terms of the life domains named in our Life-Change Inventory:

Tom's Life-Change Index = 6

1. **Mate:** Changed relationship as his wife looks for a job
2. **Health:** Anxiety and insomnia; started new medications

3. **Work:** Laid off from job
4. **Family:** Son graduated and moved to a different city
5. **Money:** Regular paycheck disappeared
6. **Home:** Moved out of home and living in small apartment

Kate's Life-Change Index = 6

1. **Mate:** Divorce became final; now single
2. **Friends:** Moved away from friends near her house
3. **Family:** Second child left for college; becoming caregiver for parents
4. **Money:** Regular paycheck ending
5. **Home:** Selling house; living with parents
6. **Work:** Layoff coming soon

Both Tom and Kate had the same Life-Change Index: 6. Yet Tom had far greater difficulty handling these changes than Kate because of their different Stress Styles. Tom's is Responsive. Kate's is Resilient. Similarly, the way you deal with change in your life depends on your Stress Style.

THE FOUR STAGES OF TRANSITION

Transition is the process of changing from one phase of life to the next. Whether changing jobs, moving to a new city, or retiring—we need to move through four stages to proceed successfully through a transition (as illustrated on page 86).

1. Relinquish: For Current Activities That Must End, Disengage and Let Go

A transition starts with some kind of pressure or demand or life change, sometimes an involuntary change, like a layoff. We must first adjust to change by letting go or *relinquishing* the past that we can't continue. This involves disengaging, ending former habits, and emotionally accepting the change. Letting go requires detaching, mourning the loss, and making emotional space to look ahead instead of backward. You must detach from the old before you can attach to the new. Letting go may involve grieving before you can consider what comes next.

2. Recess: A Time-out, a Pause to Refresh and Re-create

Between the moment of releasing the past and preparing for the future comes a pause. Maybe this hiatus lasts only an instant. In a major transition like retirement, we recommend a long enough *recess* to rest, recharge, and re-create before moving ahead. (We discuss this further in chapter 10.)

3. Redefine: Identify the Ingredients of Your New Life and Make a Plan for the Future

A successful transition enters its third stage when you actively begin to *redefine* your role by identifying your new activities and pursuits, the Ingredients of your future, and make plans to try them out.

4. Re-engage: Put Your Plan into Action

After a period of trial, learning, and practice, you can begin to reengage with confidence and to develop new habits. Once you achieve equilibrium or a stable routine, you've entered your Next Phase.

NAVIGATING YOUR LIFE TRANSITION

Understanding your Stress Style—Resilient, Mixed, or Responsive—will help in navigating your life transition. Here are some hints.

If You Have a Resilient Stress Style

Watch out for those lizards in the rearview mirror, as they may be bigger than they look. Resilient individuals often take on more than they can manage and eventually pay a price for overextending themselves.

Four Stages of Transition

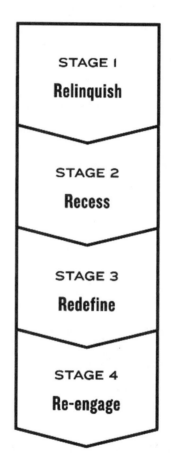

STAGE I
Relinquish

STAGE 2
Recess

STAGE 3
Redefine

STAGE 4
Re-engage

Try to empathize with those Responsive individuals close to you who don't handle stress as easily as you do. Get informed about the Responsive style to gain a better understanding of how sensitive people react to life change and stress. Remember, perception is reality!

If You Have a Responsive Stress Style

When the dinosaurs loom large, take comfort in knowing that they probably seem bigger than they are in reality. Here are five buffers to protect yourself from overwhelming stress.

TAKE TIME TO EXHALE

Breathing can measure and alter your psychological state, making a stressful moment accelerate or diminish in intensity. Oftentimes people who are anxious or upset take shallow breaths and unconsciously hold them (called inhibitory breathing). By paying attention to your breathing, particularly exhaling during tense moments, you will feel more at ease and relaxed. With practice you can even turn the stress and anxiety into excitement!

Try this breathing tip we give at seminars: Purchase a bottle of inexpensive children's bubbles (in the toy section at most stores) and use it to learn how to exhale slowly. Breathing from your abdomen, blow through the bubble blower with a steady stream of breath. If you blow too hard or too softly, you won't get any bubbles. However, you will find that smooth and steady breaths will produce a nice flow of bubbles. Use this breathing technique without the bubbles when you are feeling stressed. (If you're Resilient, you might use this technique to get in touch with the stress you're denying!)

LEARN TO MEDITATE

Meditation can help manage stress. You can learn the principles of meditation quickly, though putting them into practice takes time, discipline, and effort. The traditional way to meditate involves sitting quietly in a calm environment, focusing upon and repeating a mantra (a word such as *om*) or a prayer (the Lord's Prayer, for example), or simply following your breath and counting each inhalation (one) and exhalation (two) until you reach ten and then starting over. Whenever your mind wanders away from the mantra or your counting, simply return to it. The object is to come back without criticism and start again. With practice—twenty minutes once or twice a day—you will develop a sense of calm when meditating. Once you master this technique, you can use your mantra to ward off stress and to help you through anxious periods.

PACE YOURSELF

Setting priorities and budgeting your time can help in pacing yourself to manage stress. As you schedule your day, budget ample time for your tasks. Do first things (highest priority) first, and push off or delegate the others. Schedule breaks for recreation.

RELY ON THE SUPPORT OF OTHERS

Social support comes from your entire circle of relationships. Studies have shown that having a social network can help in coping with life change and stress. While you have little control over your Responsive Style, you can take action to cultivate a group of family members and friends who can provide emotional support.

COMMUNICATE

Finally, be patient with those Resilient individuals close to you who seem to handle stress so calmly. Realize they may have trouble seeing why you feel stressed, so communication is important to increase understanding and awareness in relationships. Resilient people don't mean to be insensitive. They are just not as sensitive to emotional nuance as you are.

As you move into your Next Phase, realize that the transition might get difficult. Some life changes will have more impact than others. For instance, redefining your relationship with your mate will have a greater emotional impact than changing your daily exercise.

In the next chapter, we'll help you identify what you're leaving behind if you leave your work. You'll find out where you find fulfillment now and where you'll look for it in your next phase. You'll also find out if you have an *Independent* Activity Style (prefer autonomy), an *Interdependent* style (prefer to cooperate), or a mixture of the two.

CHAPTER 6

What Is Your Activity Style?

How Understanding Your Activity Style Influences Your
Personal Fulfillment

DARRELL'S PASSION FOR WRITING

Coworkers describe Darrell as "the go-to guy for software questions." According to Kimberly, a branch manager at the regional bank, Darrell knew more than anyone about the inner workings of the software that ran the bank's accounting systems and Web-site services. "If I have a question about the accounting programs, I know to call Darrell. He's quiet, doesn't waste any words. When he has something to say, it's worth hearing. Give Darrell a technical problem to solve, or a difficult question, and he'll go back into his office and work on it until he figures it out. He can solve problems that stump the other software engineers. All the project managers want him on their teams, he's so sharp."

Darrell has spent much of his adult life as an employee of the bank. However, when asked if his successful IT career had been fulfilling, he responded, "I never really thought of it that way. I only work this job to pay my bills!"

Darrell added, "Of course, the bank pays well. Obviously that's important to me. I also like the flextime, because it gives me three-day weekends to work on my writing. And I like the company gym; it's really convenient to get a workout during the lunch hour. Even so, after doing the same job for thirty years, I'm more than ready for a break."

Having earned a master's degree in software engineering after his undergraduate degree in accounting, Darrell had no trouble finding the job at the bank, decades earlier. Over the years he built a reputation as a solid, technical performer and individual contributor. Every few years he received another offer to take a job as supervisor or project leader. He gently declined each promotion. "I'm not cut out for that kind of work," he said. "Programming, that's what I do best for the bank, and I prefer just to keep doing what I do well." In fact last year a national software-engineering association gave Darrell an award of excellence for one of his financial-accounting programs.

But Darrell's real passion is writing. He enjoys researching and creating science fiction. Having published two novels, Darrell was three chapters away from finishing another.

"A few months ago, I wrote to a few literary agencies, describing my current project," Darrell said. "An agent in New York City called me the day she received my letter and asked to read the completed manuscript. If I didn't need the income, I would have left this job years ago—to work full-time in my home office, writing science fiction."

Darrell has a financial plan for his new phase, which will begin in just a few months, when he turns sixty-two. With thirty years at the same bank, he plans to take early Social Security retirement along with his bank pension, and then enjoy the fulfillment he gets from his creative-writing projects.

"Sometimes I wonder if I'm making the right decision to retire so young," Darrell muses. "What will I miss about my job at the bank? I guess time will tell."

MARGARET'S OPEN-DOOR POLICY

While Darrell often kept the door to his office closed—so he could concentrate on his software projects in solitude—Margaret always left hers open, to welcome visitors. At sixty-four this marketing manager at a retail store is at the peak of her career. She likes to spend her days connecting with her store's customers, calling suppliers, visiting vendors, and cooperating with coworkers. She gets energy and ideas through interaction with others. A self-made professional, Margaret started as a salesclerk, then became a department manager, then accepted the job as marketing manager after twenty years. She attributes her promotions to her natural ability to get along with people, to communicate and cooperate—and to her open-door policy.

"I believe that life is filled with problems just waiting to be solved," Margaret said. "And if enough of us put our minds together, we can tackle the challenges together and find the best answers. I tell everyone—customers, coworkers, suppliers, and even the local media—that my door is always open. I'll make myself available any time they have a question, problem, or concern. Our job at the store is to make sure our customers are delighted with their shopping experience."

For example, last Christmas season a young mother found Margaret's office on the second floor of the store.

"I was working on the year-end marketing reports and this petite woman with twin preschool-age boys burst through my doorway and laid a note on my desk," Margaret said. "I was a little startled. Then I read the note: 'Please help me. I need two Elmo dolls by December twenty-fourth! I cannot find them anywhere.'"

Margaret asked the young woman to write down her name and phone number, and told her that "Santa" would call back soon. Margaret dropped what she was doing and called every toy distributor and retail store she knew and asked about Elmo dolls. She finally found two of them in a Seattle warehouse that someone had overlooked. The distributor sent the dolls via overnight delivery. When Margaret received the box, she immediately called the young mother, who was both grateful and relieved.

"I'm a mom and know the pressure she felt buying special gifts for her young sons," Margaret explained. "I'm also a professional and believe my job is to help meet the needs of my customers. So I always dig until I find the best answers."

As Margaret shared more stories about her open-door policy and the many people whose lives she had touched through the years, she mentioned her upcoming retirement. "I've considered retiring now that I'm sixty-four, but I worry that I will miss my work and the people I see each day. I've asked myself what will give me as much enjoyment as I've gotten here at the store?"

WHAT MAKES YOU HAPPY?

Have you ever considered what it takes for you to feel satisfied and contented? What you enjoy doing so much that you lose track of time? Maybe you thrive on teamwork and feel satisfied when you're doing your part of a big, difficult project with your teammates, and share high fives when you get done. Maybe you get so wrapped up in a creative solo project that you forget to look at the clock and work straight through the day without a break. Or perhaps you crave physical challenge, such as walking an extra lap or running that extra mile. Then again, maybe making money brings you fulfillment and gives you a way to gauge your accomplishments.

What if we asked you to identify the sources of fulfillment in your work or career? Would you have to stop and think? People often aren't aware of the various kinds of satisfaction they receive from their work . . . until it's too late. When they do stop work, they feel confident at first that they will "thrive in retirement" — only to realize later that they miss what they've left behind.

After you take the third Personality Quiz (page 94) and find out if you're Independent, Interdependent, or Mixed, we'll help you identify the sources of fulfillment in your life up to now. Armed with awareness of your Activity Style, and knowing what you've found important and satisfying in your work and life, you can select pursuits for your retirement that will bring fulfillment.

FULFILLMENT = SATISFACTION + IMPORTANCE

Fulfillment comes when you find satisfaction from doing what's important to you. It has two necessary ingredients: *satisfaction* and *importance*. As an example, Margaret felt *satisfied* when she could help customers find what they wanted at the store, as she did by locating the young mother's Elmo dolls. Margaret regarded it as *important* to serve her customers; she placed a very high value on helping and supporting the people around her. So, as a result, Margaret found it personally fulfilling to serve her customers, because she gained satisfaction from doing what she valued and considered important. In fact Margaret often saw herself in the role of a parent or counselor as people came to her with their personal problems. She empathized with them, listened, and then tried to help them find what they sought. Margaret derived much satisfaction from being of service, and because it represented a personal value, she found great fulfillment from that aspect of her work.

Activities that fail to provide one of the key ingredients—satisfaction or importance—eventually prove unfulfilling. For example, Margaret's job as a manager gave her power and influence through the decisions she made—about who would serve as the store's suppliers, which product lines it would carry, and so on. For her the power and authority of her position represented necessary duties, more like unpleasant chores than sources of satisfaction. She regarded the decision-making part of her job as important, but for her, exercising power and influencing people through her decisions was not satisfying: an unfulfilling part of her job.

Remember how Darrell said he "works to pay his bills"? He felt satisfied with his salary from the job, and earning was very important to him—at least until his pension replaces his paycheck. So Darrell found his job fulfilling as a source of earning. However, while he felt satisfied with his software, he didn't consider his software engineering important. Because designing software wasn't important to Darrell, even though he felt satisfied with his

PERSONALITY QUIZ #3: WHAT IS YOUR ACTIVITY STYLE? INDEPENDENT VS. INTERDEPENDENT

Consider how you think, feel, and act *most of the time* when away from work and free to be yourself. Mark each statement *true* or *false*. If a statement is sometimes true and other times false, mark it *true* if it describes you even *slightly* more often than not. Avoid responses based on your work role or what others expect or how you'd like to be. If in doubt, go with your *first reaction* or *intuition*.

True	False	
❏	❏	1. When the going gets tough, the tough get help.
❏	❏	2. My proudest achievements come from great teamwork.
❏	❏	3. Two heads are much better than one.
❏	❏	4. I'd rather start a new project as a member of a group than by myself.
❏	❏	5. I've found nothing more satisfying than working with like-minded people.
❏	❏	6. In a group effort, I trust that all will do their share.
❏	❏	7. There is strength in numbers.
❏	❏	8. Cooperating with just about anyone comes naturally for me.
❏	❏	9. I enjoy being a team player.
❏	❏	10. I find it easy to put common goals before my own.
_____		My total score (count the number of boxes marked *true*)

What Your Score Means

A score of 7, 8, 9, or 10 indicates an Interdependent Activity Style—the higher the score, the more consistent your preference. *A score of 4, 5, or 6 indicates a Mixed Interdependent / Independent Activity Style. A score of 0, 1, 2, or 3 shows an Independent Activity Style*—the lower the score, the more consistent your preference for that style.

Interdependent Activity Style (7–10): You tend to prefer cooperative activities and like to work in concert with others. You prefer collaboration to individual efforts and place a high value on teamwork. You function best by joining the process and helping to create agreement. You may find it uncomfortable to work by yourself.

Mixed Independent/Interdependent Activity Style (4–6): You tend to enjoy both individual and solo projects, as well as teamwork and collaboration. Depending on the situation, you might like an individual, self-sufficient pursuit or prefer to join a cooperative effort. You may try to combine or alternate the two styles if you can manage it.

Independent Activity Style (7–10): You tend to prefer autonomous, individual activities and like to rely on your own efforts; you value self-sufficiency. In a group or team, you might see yourself as having to pull more than your own weight. You function best on your own when you can control your own activity—or direct the activities of others. You may find it uncomfortable to accept direction or constraint from others.

Your Personality Profile

Record your Activity Style (Interdependent, Mixed, or Independent) on the Personality Profile module below. Then turn to the last chapter in the book, where you'll find your Personality

Profile showing all seven traits (page 185). Record the result for your Activity Style there, too, to review later.

My Activity Style

ACTIVITY

INDEPENDENT	MIXED	INTERDEPENDENT
Self-directed. Needs autonomy. Likes to work solo or lead.	Likes some independence and some cooperation. Can lead or follow.	Prefers cooperation, teamwork, collaboration, and consensus.

programs, software engineering was unfulfilling as a source of personal accomplishment.

Margaret and Darrell appreciated different things about their jobs and found different sources of fulfillment in their work. These differences illustrate the personal, subjective nature of each individual's fulfillment, which became especially obvious in their opposite experiences with physical exercise. Darrell genuinely enjoyed his daily lunch-hour workout at the company gym. In contrast, Margaret did not look forward to exercising. For Margaret fulfillment came from the social connection she built into her exercise routine by walking with friends and coworkers.

MEASURING FULFILLMENT

We sought to gauge how much personal fulfillment people *stand to lose by retiring from work.* This called for listing potential sources of satisfaction—from work and elsewhere—for anyone. After doing extensive research and questioning dozens of retirees, we developed a list of twenty sources. It appears in Your Fulfillment Quiz (page 104).

The quiz asks, for each source: is this *satisfying?* Is it *important?* Has it come *mostly from work?* Based on the answers, it quantifies fulfillment from work as a ratio of the number of sources mainly from work (satisfying *and* important) to the total number of sources from all of life, including work.

After reading Darrell's and Margaret's responses, you can take the quiz to see how much fulfillment you'll lose by retiring.

Darrell's Sources of Fulfillment That Came Mostly from Work

- *Physical exercise:* Important + Satisfying. Daily, lunchtime workouts at the company gym.
- *Earning:* Important + Satisfying. Main reason for the job. (Won't be important after retirement.)
- *Professional affiliation:* Important + Satisfying. Participating in task forces in professional software-engineering associations. Representing the bank at professional conferences with colleagues in software engineering.
- *Social connection:* Important + Satisfying. Connecting with other employees and vendors through cooperation on project teams at the bank.
- *Friendship:* Important + Satisfying. A few close, long-standing friendships at work.

Some of Darrell's Sources of Fulfillment That Did Not Come Mostly from Work

- *Creative expression:* Important + Satisfying. Away from the job. Most satisfying creative effort: researching and writing science fiction at home. Less creative—actually easy—and not nearly as satisfying: designing accounting software.
- *Family:* Important + Satisfying. At home. Time with wife, children, grandchildren.
- *Independent accomplishment:* Important + Satisfying. Most gratifying, independent achievements: getting short stories and novels published. Satisfying, but not important: software projects well done; awards for software engineering.
- *Self-Development:* Important + Satisfying. Away from work: reading and research for science fiction. Writers' workshops. College classes on science in the evening school at the university. Some at work: learning new programming languages, attending software-engineering workshops.
- *Time structure:* Important + Satisfying. Organizing my time comes easily; I don't depend on my job to do that for me.

Darrell's Fulfillment Quiz			
Source of Personal Fulfillment	Satisfying to me?	Important to me?	Mostly from work?
1. Recognition	X	X	
2. Time structure	X	X	
3. Purpose	X	X	
4. Helping others	X		
5. Community	X	X	
6. Family	X	X	
7. Professional affiliation	X	X	X
8. Mental challenge	X	X	
9. Physical exercise	X	X	X
10. Influence			
11. Collaboration	X		X
12. Earning	X	X	X
13. Creative expression	X	X	
14. Environments	X	X	
15. Independent accomplishment	X	X	
16. Social connection	X	X	X
17. Travel	X		
18. Spirituality	X		
19. Self-development	X	X	
20. Friendship	X	X	X
# Fulfilling: (Count # Satisfying + Important)	15		
# Fulfilling Mostly from Work (Count # with all columns marked)			5

Margaret's Main Sources of Fulfillment Mostly from Work

• *Helping Others:* Satisfying + Very Important to me! Mostly from work, off-the-job too. Biggest satisfaction: serving my customers. Serving my staff, the people I supervise, by leading them well. Being of help to coworkers, suppliers, vendors, new people I get to meet.

• *Collaboration:* Satisfying + Important. Cooperating with staff team of eight department managers (my family at the store). Serving customers. Planning promotions with our suppliers. Working with the advertising team. Public-relations partnerships. Working with charities like the American Heart Association.

• *Social connection:* Satisfying + Important. Getting to know my customers; meeting new people at the store. Networking with marketing people at other organizations. Being with coworkers, suppliers, vendors, new people I get to meet. My walk-at-the-mall friends.

• *Purpose:* Important + Satisfying. Work gives me purpose. Main reason to get up in the morning.

• *Earning:* Important + Satisfying. Job at the store is one of two family incomes.

Some of Margaret's Sources of Fulfillment That Did Not Come Mostly from Work

• *Family:* Satisfying + Important. At home: time with my husband, children now living by themselves. Babysitting grandchildren. Family get-togethers with my brothers and sisters and extended family. Neighbors like family to me.

• *Community:* Satisfying + Important. Mostly away from work: serving on the board of directors of our neighborhood homeowners association. Helping organize holiday events in our neighborhood. American Heart Association local chapter.

Margaret's Fulfillment Quiz			
Source of Personal Fulfillment	Satisfying to me?	Important to me?	Mostly from work?
1. Recognition	X		
2. Time structure	X	X	X
3. Purpose	X	X	X
4. Helping others	X	X	X
5. Community	X	X	
6. Family	X	X	
7. Professional affiliation	X	X	X
8. Mental challenge	X	X	X
9. Physical exercise		X	
10. Influence		X	
11. Collaboration	X	X	X
12. Earning	X	X	X
13. Creative expression			
14. Environments	X		
15. Independent accomplishment			
16. Social connection	X	X	X
17. Travel	X	X	X
18. Spirituality		X	
19. Self-development		X	
20. Friendship	X	X	
# Fulfilling: (Count # Satisfying + Important)	12		
# Fulfilling Mostly from Work (Count # with all columns marked)			9

WHAT BRINGS YOU FULFILLMENT?

As you look ahead to starting a new phase, you'll need to find pursuits that provide both satisfaction and importance to have fulfillment. One without the other is not enough!

A good illustration concerns earning money during retirement. Some people don't want to continue earning an income after they retire; they prefer to spend their time doing other things. Yet, for some, even though they have plenty of money, continuing to earn is a way of "keeping score," or knowing they are successful. Take Rich, fifty-six, who owns a truck-leasing conglomerate in the Midwest. He amassed more wealth than he'll ever need in a lifetime, but he wants to spend his Next Phase doing what he does best: *making money.*

In contrast, making money is no longer important to Darrell. He carefully saved money from each paycheck to put aside in his company 401(k). Along with Social Security and his bank's pension fund, Darrell feels confident that he will live comfortably without earning income from what he does in his new phase.

Your Fulfillment Quiz

Answer the questions in the Fulfillment Quiz (page 104) and review your responses. Using a different-colored marker or pen, circle the sources you marked *both* satisfying and important (in the first and second columns). These represent your personal sources of fulfillment. Count the number of circled sources, and put this number in the box at the bottom on page 105 next to # Fulfilling (be sure to count just the number marked *both* satisfying and important).

Next, count the number of sources with *all three* columns marked. Put this number in the box at the bottom of page 105 next to # Fulfilling Mostly from Work (count the number with all columns marked).

WHAT SHARE OF YOUR PERSONAL FULFILLMENT HAS COME FROM WORK?

In our seminars, participants are often surprised to learn how much of their personal fulfillment comes from their work. Some see a number as high as 75 percent (as Margaret did) and say, "I never realized how much I get from my job!" And some see a number down around 33 percent (as Darrell did) and say, "No wonder I'm ready to retire, I'm getting most of my fulfillment outside of work!"

Are you curious to know what fraction of your personal fulfillment has come mostly from your work? That's one of the two main reasons for completing the quiz. We'll help you create your Work Fulfillment Pie Chart. It shows the slice of your fulfillment pie that you have received mostly from work, if the whole pie is the combined fulfillment you received from all sources, including work and the rest of your life (work plus nonwork).

It takes five quick steps to fill in your pie chart to show the *percent of your fulfillment that has come from your career.*

1. Write the number of sources in the Fulfillment Quiz for which you marked *both* of the first two columns. This is the same number you wrote in the box at the bottom of page 105 next to # Fulfilling (count # Satisfying + Important).
   A. _____

2. Write the number of sources for which you marked *all three* columns. This is the same number you wrote in the box at the bottom of page 105 next to # Fulfilling Mostly from Work (count # with all columns marked).
   B. _____

3. Divide (B) by (A), or the # Fulfilling Mostly from Work / # Fulfilling
   C: (B/A) = _____

4. Round the fraction (B/A) to two decimal places (example, 3/12 = ¼ = .25) D: _____

FULFILLMENT QUIZ

Consider these sources of fulfillment you may have enjoyed while working. If you no longer have a full-time career, answer for when you did. For each source, answer these three questions by marking the appropriate box.

You can mark one, two, or all three boxes for each source—or none if it doesn't apply to you.

Sources of Fulfillment	Satisfying to me?	Important to me?	Mostly from work?
1. **Recognition:** having people acknowledge and appreciate what I do.	❏	❏	❏
2. **Time structure:** having duties, responsibilities, and commitments that organize my days.	❏	❏	❏
3. **Purpose:** knowing that what I do has meaning, value, and significance for myself and/or others.	❏	❏	❏
4. **Helping others:** providing service; nurturing, mentoring, assisting, and/or supporting people.	❏	❏	❏
5. **Community:** actively participating in civic projects, associations, organizations.	❏	❏	❏
6. **Family:** enjoying time with loved ones: my mate, children, siblings, family, and/or relatives.	❏	❏	❏
7. **Professional affiliation:** regular interaction with others involved in the kind of work I do.	❏	❏	❏
8. **Mental challenge:** intellectual excitement; pursuits that engage, stretch, and sharpen my mind.	❏	❏	❏
9. **Physical exercise:** activity that requires walking, lifting, carrying, etc.; regular exercise for fun and fitness.	❏	❏	❏

Sources of Fulfillment	Satisfying to me?	Important to me?	Mostly from work?
10. **Influence:** exercising power, authority, or leadership in what I do; having status.	❏	❏	❏
11. **Collaboration:** cooperating in joint efforts; working and/or playing as a member of a team, committee, or group.	❏	❏	❏
12. **Earning:** generating income from my efforts; being paid for what I do.	❏	❏	❏
13. **Creative expression:** generating original ideas, products, art, performances, or knowledge; designing solutions or systems.	❏	❏	❏
14. **Environments:** functional, pleasing places that give needed comfort, solitude, interaction, and/or stimulation.	❏	❏	❏
15. **Independent accomplishment:** individual achievement through sustained, personal effort.	❏	❏	❏
16. **Social connection:** networking; staying in touch, informed, and up-to-date via personal contacts.	❏	❏	❏
17. **Travel:** journeying to visit (or revisit) distant, enjoyable places.	❏	❏	❏
18. **Spirituality:** participation in church, worship, religion, or introspection.	❏	❏	❏
19. **Self-development:** lifelong learning, education, training, or study.	❏	❏	❏
20. **Friendship:** spending time and relaxing with my friends and companions.	❏	❏	❏
# Fulfilling: (Count # Satisfying + Important)			
# Fulfilling Mostly from Work: (Count # with all columns marked)			

Sample Fulfillment Pie Charts

Darrell's Chart Shows 33 Percent of His Personal Fulfillment Mostly from Work

Margaret's Chart Shows 75 Percent of Her Personal Fulfillment Mostly from Work

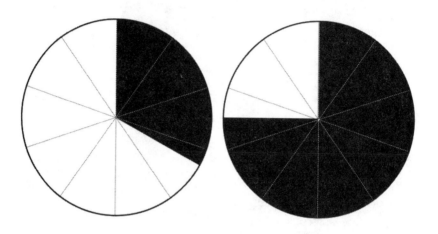

Darrell, 33%   *Margaret, 75%*

5. Now using the blank pie chart on page 107, fill in the appropriate slice of the pie to show the share of fulfillment you receive from work (D). (You can see Darrell's and Margaret's pie charts above as examples.)

Besides learning how much fulfillment comes from your work, another reason for completing the Fulfillment Quiz is to identify your *specific sources of personal fulfillment* up to now. Many of our clients are surprised to see how long their lists of sources are and how many involve their work. Once you know what

My Fulfillment Pie Chart

(Fill in the Slices to Show the Percent of Fulfillment Mostly from Work,

From: # Fulfilling Mostly from Work / # Fulfilling)

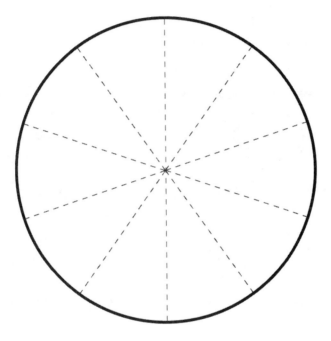

has fulfilled you in the past, you can make a mindful decision about what you'll seek in your future. And the key questions have to do with your Activity Style: Will you seek fulfillment from cooperative pursuits and helping others as Margaret did? Or will you seek solitary pursuits more focused on independent accomplishment and self-development as Darrell did? Or will you seek some combination? Before answering, consider your Activity Style.

FINDING FULFILLMENT THAT FITS *YOUR* PERSONALITY

Personality traits influence what we find fulfilling; Activity Style relates specifically to our preferred mix of teamwork and self-directed pursuits. Both Darrell and Margaret sought fulfillment that matched their personalities.

Darrell's Independent Activity Style

Darrell prefers working solo, so he chose a career based mainly on solitary work, designing software. Besides independent accomplishment, other sources of fulfillment that match his Independent Activity Style include creative expression, from writing at home, and physical exercise, from working out by himself at the gym.

Margaret's Interdependent Activity Style

With her Interdependent Activity Style, Margaret feels drawn to co-operative pursuits. Margaret described her career in marketing and customer service as "an extended team effort with my family at the store." She finds much fulfillment in consensus building, teamwork, and helping others by nurturing, supporting, or mentoring them.

NOW CONSIDER THESE KEY QUESTIONS ABOUT YOUR NEXT PHASE

Success in your Next Phase depends on your decisions about your sources of personal fulfillment. Consider the following questions:

1. In your Next Phase, how much fulfillment will come from your work?

Make this decision mindfully. Don't turn your back on your career until you know what you're leaving behind. For example, Darrell realized that his work provided most of his social connection, and that he could maintain much of it by continuing to work part-time instead of leaving his job completely.

2. Whether or not you leave your job, what sources of fulfillment from your work will you continue to seek?

Identify the sources of fulfillment from your work you'll try to replace when and if you leave it. For instance, Margaret knows that much of her personal fulfillment has come from her relationships with people at work. She sees that her Next Phase will have to involve cooperation and service to others. Wherever she goes next, she'll look for the same kinds of fulfillment she has enjoyed at the store.

3. What new sources of fulfillment, if any, will you seek now that you haven't before?

Even if you like your job, maybe you'll want to do something entirely different. For instance, Margaret talked about going back to school, perhaps to learn counseling. "My job never left time for self-development!" If you do consider something new, make sure it suits your Activity Style.

To find your best future, you'll have to do the homework. It calls for understanding your personality and the sources of fulfillment you'll want in your Next Phase. In the next chapter, we'll help you look back for memories and forward for dreams that might suggest options for your Next Phase. With some creative brainstorming, you can find many possibilities to explore—and later choose the best ones for your personality.

CHAPTER 7

What Is Your Information Style?

How Understanding Your Information Style Will Help You
Brainstorm Options for Retirement

CHARLES'S QUESTION

Charles was reading an editorial in the *Columbus Dispatch* when he heard Colleen calling. Divorced for more than a decade, Charles had met Colleen, fifty-three, while traveling in England five years earlier. They continued to date afterward, and Colleen moved in with Charles last year.

"Charles, Peter sent us an e-mail!" Colleen said from the computer room.

Charles's son, Peter, twenty-three, had graduated from Purdue University and moved to Dayton to start his first full-time job as a mechanical engineer. In an e-mail to Charles and Colleen, he wrote:

> *Hey! How's it going? I just finished my first week at a real job and wanted to thank you guys for all the emotional (and financial!) support. I can't believe that I'm doing something I love and getting paid for it.*
>
> *Dad, what's up with you? You've been with the county a long time now. What about retiring?*

With a master's degree in statistics, Charles had worked as a statistician for a county government in Ohio for twenty-seven years, and enjoyed his career and tenure. But he felt clueless when it came to the Next Phase of his life.

Later that night Charles thought about Peter's question: "What about retiring?" He'd made a secure niche for himself at the county and could easily work there another decade or longer. Perhaps he should move to Phoenix, where his elderly mother lived. He and Colleen could buy a house together. His friend in the Arizona state government had lately asked him to apply for an open position in Phoenix as a statistician. On the other hand, maybe he should use this opportunity to go back to school and get a PhD in statistics; he had his eye on a particular doctoral program. Then Charles remembered the job that Mick, a college friend, had offered him last year. "I guarantee you fewer hours and a lot more money than you're making now," Mick had said. "Just say the word, and you've got the job." Charles wasn't sure what the job entailed, but he could find out.

Is it becoming obvious that Charles wants to keep working? After all, he mentioned only career-related options. Charles, with his Practical Information Style, looked to well-known precedents and established, familiar pathways. He had a specific list of concrete options. For Charles and others with a Practical Information Style, looking beyond the familiar or far into the future can prove difficult.

As he went to bed, Charles promised himself he would talk to Colleen about retirement in the morning, and look into attending an upcoming retirement workshop for county employees.

Maybe you dream of a new career after retirement but don't know how to begin finding options that fit for you. Or perhaps you're looking for something entirely new to do in retirement—a total break from the career or industry where you've spent your working life so far. How you see your options depends on your Information Style, or the way you perceive, learn, and organize information from the world. Your Information Style determines whether you feel more comfortable looking to your past experience (a Practical Information Style, which Charles demonstrates) or whether you prefer to envision future possibilities (a Visionary Information Style).

In this chapter we'll give you a chance to identify your Information Style, Practical vs. Visionary. Armed with this information, we will help you brainstorm options for your Next Phase. We'll introduce you to some fun, creative tools—collage and a lifeline—and guide you in using them to stimulate thinking of possible options for the future.

PROGRESS REVIEW

Before you do the next Personality Quiz (next page), here's a review of what you have learned about yourself so far. From the previous personality quizzes, you identified three traits for your Personality Profile (on page 185):

- **Your Social Style** — Outgoing, Contemplative, or Mixed — and your social needs (chapter 4).
- **Your Stress Style** — Resilient, Responsive, or Mixed — and how you manage the stress of life change (chapter 5).
- **Your Activity Style** — Interdependent, Independent, or Mixed — and the combination of cooperative and solo pursuits you want in your life (chapter 6).

You've also evaluated the amount of change in your life by completing the Life-Change Inventory and then computing your Life-Change Index (chapter 5). Then you estimated how much of your personal fulfillment has come from your work by completing the Fulfillment Quiz and creating your Fulfillment Pie Chart (chapter 6).

PAMELA'S VISIONARY APPROACH TO SEEING OPTIONS

"When I started nursing school, I saw my lifelong dream of helping others coming true," said Pamela, fifty-five. "And it seemed perfect for many years — until I accepted a promotion and got frustrated with nursing."

It looked to her like a dream job. Then on Pamela's first day she ran into the realities. "We had a patient in every bed, and we were understaffed. I've scrambled ever since to hire nurses and assistants. As soon as I got one trained, another would quit because of the workload. The staff couldn't handle the number of patients on

PERSONALITY QUIZ #4:
WHAT IS YOUR INFORMATION STYLE?
PRACTICAL VS. VISIONARY

Consider how you think, feel, and act *most of the time* when away from work and free to be yourself. Mark each statement *true* or *false*. If a statement is sometimes true and other times false, mark it *true* if it describes you even *slightly* more often than not. Avoid responses based on your work role or what others expect or how you'd like to be. If in doubt, go with your *first reaction* or *intuition*.

True **False**

❑ ❑ 1. I tend to see the trees before I notice the forest.

❑ ❑ 2. I would rather teach a class about bicycle repair than about psychology.

❑ ❑ 3. When I face a new problem, I look first for solutions that have worked in the past.

❑ ❑ 4. My friends value my common-sense suggestions.

❑ ❑ 5. I find comfort in traditions.

❑ ❑ 6. Keep your theory, and show me a real-life example!

❑ ❑ 7. I am loyal to what's tried and true.

❑ ❑ 8. Vague ideas and suggestions annoy me.

❑ ❑ 9. Abstract, philosophical discussions don't interest me.

❑ ❑ 10. In any new situation, I pay careful attention to the facts and details.

_____ My total score (count the number of boxes marked *true*)

What Your Score Means

A score of 7, 8, 9, or 10 indicates a Practical style—the higher the score, the more consistent your preference for the Practical style. *A score of 4, 5, or 6 indicates a Mixed Practical/Visionary style. A score of 0, 1, 2, or 3 shows a Visionary Information Style*—the lower the score, the more consistent your preference for this style.

Practical Information Style (7–10): You tend to value tried-and-true ways of doing things, hands-on experience, and commonsense solutions. You usually mistrust untested or vague ideas and prefer to rely on precedent and direct experience. You pay attention to detail and tend to find solace in tradition. Innovation and change can make you uncomfortable. You prefer to plan in small steps and don't readily think too far ahead. You may find long-term planning difficult.

Mixed Practical/Visionary Information Style (4–6): You have equal affinity for the new and novel as for the proven and familiar. Depending on the circumstances, you strive for balance between tradition and innovation. You can see the big picture as well as the details. You have some facility with both abstract ideas and concrete facts.

Visionary Information Style (0–3): You tend to envision possibilities and see the big picture. You value innovation and new learning, and find motivation in novelty and variety. At ease with theory and abstraction, you relish new learning and change for its own sake. You get easily bored by too many details, and you may overlook concrete problems and practical realities.

Your Personality Profile

Record your Information Style (Practical, Mixed, or Visionary) on your Personality Profile module below. Then turn to the last chapter in the book, where you'll find your Personality Profile showing all seven traits (page 185). Record the result for your Activity Style there, too.

My Information Style

PRACTICAL	INFORMATION	VISIONARY
	MIXED	
Detail-oriented. Trusts experience. Prefers precedent over innovation.	Sees big picture and details. Focuses on precedents and possibilities.	Big-picture-oriented. Easily envisions possibilities. Misses details.

the floor. I signed up to help people, but I found myself in a system that didn't deliver the care our patients deserved. I was ready to give up nursing."

Then Pamela's former roommate from nursing school, Wanda, made a surprise visit. "Wanda's a registered psychiatric nurse. She saw I was depressed and burned out," Pamela said. "She asked if I wanted to talk about it. Did I ever!"

Remember the Fulfillment Quiz from chapter 6? This quiz identified two necessary ingredients of personal fulfillment: *satisfaction* from doing what's *important*. While helping others was important to Pamela, trying to help patients as nursing supervisor had proven unsatisfying. Lacking one of the two necessary ingredients, as Pamela did, leads to feeling unfulfilled—exactly how Pamela felt.

Wanda suggested Pamela consider moving to Canada to continue her nursing career. "We have more nurses on the floor and a lower patient load at Toronto General. I know of some openings in pediatrics. You could stay with me until you find a place to live."

The two friends chatted about relocating to Toronto, and Pamela wrote the suggestion on a legal pad. They discussed other options—some outlandish and even fanciful—that Pamela had kept to herself over the past few months. Maybe she could go to cooking school. Or investigate a Teaching Fellows program she'd read about that trained professionals to be public-school teachers. Perhaps she could even take some time off from work and seize the opportunity to travel in South America, as she'd dreamed of doing. She wrote those ideas down, too.

After Wanda left, Pamela continued to brainstorm options and add to her list of possibilities for her Next Phase. Her Visionary Style made it much easier for her to envision possibilities in the abstract than to deal with day-to-day realities. Pamela promised herself she would carefully evaluate any options she might consider for her future.

CHARLES'S PRACTICAL APPROACH TO SEEING OPTIONS

When Charles thought ahead to his life at retirement, he immediately looked to the past. With his Practical Information Style he first considered his experiences—as a statistician, his educational background in statistics, and even extending what he had done before by working for his friend Mick. Charles's information style led him to see options by *building on his experience.* As you'll read later in this chapter, Charles used creative tools to tap his memories for options.

LOOK BACK AND DREAM FORWARD FOR MEMORIES AND DREAMS

In helping people generate and explore options for their futures, we have found that the best place to start is in your own life—in past experiences and personal dreams or hopes. Some people start by looking at the long lists of possibilities readily available in books and on Web sites. Eventually they realize they'll have to sort out what fits for them personally, so they go back to their own lives as the point of reference. We suggest you start there, and work forward from a list of specific memories and dreams.

Make your lists of memories and dreams in two steps. In each step you make a separate list, and eventually combine them:

Step 1: Look Back—for your list of *Memories*
Step 2: Dream Forward—for your list of *Dreams*

Your Information Style determines which step to do first: the one in your comfort zone. Then take a break and do the other step— the one you can expect to find more difficult. When you've done both steps, combine them into a list of memories and dreams to use in generating possible options for your future.

- If you have a Practical Information Style: *Look Back* first and then *Dream Forward*.
- If you have a Visionary Information Style: *Dream Forward* first and then *Look Back*.
- If you have a Mixed Information Style: you likely have a slight preference for one of the two approaches; do the one that calls to you.

Look Back (for Memories)

In this activity you make a list of memories to stimulate ideas about possible options for the future. First, jog your memory by looking at old appointment books, calendars, journals, or photo albums— or talk with older relatives, neighbors, teachers, and friends.

Start your list of memories by answering the following questions with a few words each. Try for two or three memories per question.

1. What did you enjoy doing in your most recent workweek? (Examples: made a great presentation to the sales team, prepared an excellent gourmet meal, finished a spreadsheet that balanced on the first try, performed perfect laser eye surgery, organized a computer database, or finished writing a document.)
2. What activities did you enjoy in your most recent weekend?

(Examples: went running with a friend, toured an art museum with children, refinished an antique, met friends at a restaurant, read a book, watched sports on TV, went to a movie.)

3. *What activities did you enjoy on your most recent vacation?* (Examples: trail hiking, learning how to sail a boat, touring castles in Scotland, white-water rafting, visiting old college friends, relaxing on the beach.)

4. *What interests or talents did you have as a child?* (Examples: Little League baseball, tap dancing, writing plays for friends to perform, building furniture, bringing homeless animals to my house, operating a ham radio, catching fireflies.)

5. *What classes in school did you find most intriguing?* (Examples: logic and set theory, creative writing, geography, physical education, chorus.)

6. *What extracurricular activities did you enjoy in high school and college?* (Examples: service clubs, newspaper staff, yearbook staff, student government, athletic teams, sororities and fraternities.)

7. *What were some of your happiest times as a teenager and young adult?* (Examples: vacations, camping, dating, college years, first car, first job.)

8. *What are your most satisfying achievements?* (Examples: marriage, children, alumnus award, achievement awards at work, community honors, first home, watching family members achieve.)

9. *What are the proudest moments of your life?* (Examples: birth of child, kids' graduations, weight loss, being asked to serve as a trustee, running a marathon, publishing an article or book, getting a promotion or raise, professional award or honor.)

SAMPLE ITEMS FROM CHARLES'S LIST OF MEMORIES

- Playing tennis in college
- Using a telescope to see the planets
- Riding bikes with neighbors
- Practicing putting at a nearby golf course

- Practicing violin
- Catching snakes in the canal behind grandparents' country home
- Working at my uncle's feed-and-seed store
- Getting my first calculator in middle school

Dream Forward (for Hopes)

In this activity make a long list of dreams or hopes—things you've always wanted to do, or what you're doing now and want to continue in your new phase. For inspiration talk with people close to you and look at old journals, letters, and e-mail you have saved.

To start your list of dreams, answer the following questions with a few words each. Try to write down two or three items per question.

1. *What have you always hoped to achieve?* (Examples: write a book, climb Mountain Everest, walk the Appalachian Trail, recite a poem in French at the top of the Eiffel Tower, learn to knit, bake bread, play piano.)

2. *What have you wanted to do with people closest to you but haven't found time to do yet?* (Examples: teach my kids piano, cook a gourmet meal together, help my kids start a business, travel abroad as a family, take my grandkids camping.)

3. *What activities have you put off and hoped to find time to do?* (Examples: sing in the community chorus, take my granddaughter fishing, go to a professional football game, go scuba diving, ski in Colorado, ride in the space shuttle.)

4. *What talents or skills have you always hoped to develop?* (Examples: golf, ballroom dancing, oil painting, woodworking, calligraphy, knitting, gourmet cooking.)

5. *What places do you hope to go?* (Examples: Alaska, Hawaii, Rome, Samoa, Sweden, Austria.)

6. *What individuals would you like to know better?* (Examples:

neighbors, in-laws, our rabbi, the mayor, Condoleezza Rice, the Dalai Lama.)

7. *What would you like to learn about, or what classes would you take first if you went back to school, this time without getting graded?* (Examples: politics, the environment, alternative-medicine therapies, acupuncture, car maintenance, economics, world religions, a new language.)

8. *What activities do you want to do with people close to you that you hope to continue in the future?* (Examples: exercise with my spouse, take our granddaughter to breakfast on Saturdays, worship with our family, give our annual holiday open house for neighbors, work on a political campaign with our son.)

9. *What do you hope to do in your career that you haven't done yet?* (Examples: start a business, be a mentor, work from a home-based office, move into a supervisory position, volunteer to teach young students about my career.)

10. *How would you like to contribute, make a difference, or have people remember you?* (Examples: run for political office, serve on the school board, teach classes at church, write a screenplay, direct a musical production.)

PAMELA'S LIST OF DREAMS

- Help house the homeless
- Organize a soup kitchen for the homeless at my church
- Become a pediatric nurse at Toronto General Hospital
- Become a navy medic
- Become a foster parent for HIV newborns
- Become a public-health nurse at an elementary school
- Work in a private pediatric practice
- Learn to skydive
- Move to Berkeley, California (where Pamela's two brothers live)
- Train for a marathon

- Work on a medical team for a major cruise line
- Work at a hospital in England
- Give powerful speeches on human rights to packed auditoriums
- Lead a parade of like-minded individuals in an effort to conquer poverty
- Work at a medical spa in California
- Go to divinity school
- Become ordained as a Unitarian minister
- Join the Peace Corps

Now Combine Your Lists of Memories and Dreams

Before you proceed, combine the two lists you have just made. Now you have your combined lists of memories and dreams. You'll use it as a starting point to generate possible options for your future in the next step, *brainstorming.*

BRAINSTORM YOUR OPTIONS FOR THE FUTURE

Brainstorming offers the best tool we've found for tapping creativity. You can work solo or with a friend or in a group, whichever feels most comfortable. If you have an Outgoing Social Style, we suggest you work with a few friends; if you have a Contemplative Social Style, we suggest you find a quiet place to write in your journal. Either way, you'll need some paper and a pen or pencil.

1. Start with the first memory or dream from the list you made earlier. If you have a Practical Information Style, write down your first memory. If you have a Visionary Information Style, write down your first dream.

Examples:
Charles' first memory: *playing tennis in college*
Pamela's first dream: *help house the homeless*

2. Now brainstorm and list all the possible options you can think of from the memory or dream. These options consist of creative ways you could build on that memory or realize that dream. How can you make your memory relevant again or your dream a reality?

Examples:

Charles's List of Options That Build on "Playing Tennis in College"

- Take private tennis lessons
- Play tennis with son
- Read a book on tennis
- Coach tennis
- Referee tennis
- Travel to World Cup tennis matches
- Write a book on tennis
- Buy a tennis club
- Build a vacation villa in the South of France with a tennis court
- Work at a tennis club
- Work in a sports store
- Collect tennis racquets
- Go to a tennis camp
- Build a tennis court
- Learn to string tennis racquets

Pamela's List of Options for "Help House the Homeless"

- Start an advocacy organization for homeless shelters
- Start a homeless shelter downtown
- Raise funds to open and run a subsidized hotel for the homeless

- Start an endowed fund for grants to promote housing for the homeless
- Volunteer in a homeless shelter
- Volunteer at a food bank
- Volunteer at a soup kitchen
- Organize a citywide petition to allocate more funds for the homeless
- Volunteer to write grants for agencies helping the homeless
- Invite a homeless person to spend the night in the spare bedroom
- Become "homeless" for a month

3. Follow these four brainstorming rules as you're generating options for each memory or dream:

- *Rule #1: Speed. Go as fast as you can!* (Don't overthink or you'll end up with writer's block.)
- *Rule #2: Quantity. Go for numbers!* List as many ideas as you can think of. (If you have more than fifty, that's okay, keep going. No limits.)
- *Rule #3: Don't Evaluate.* Suspend judgment. Free your mind! Liberate your creative spirit from the shackles of self-editing . . . or self-doubt. All ideas are okay now. Evaluate later.
- *Rule #4: Piggyback!* Build on previous ideas. Add one or two extra-wild-and-crazy ideas. Let yourself go. Have fun.

4. Repeat this process for each memory or dream. *Be sure to follow the four rules of brainstorming!* Resist the urge to cross things off or edit. Don't even ask yourself if it's possible; just write it down and move on! Write something impossible to get into the spirit of brainstorming!

Remember the five keys for a successful retirement (page 14) discussed in chapter 1? When you finish brainstorming creative options for all your memories and dreams, look back over your list and make sure you have included a few options for the first four keys (the fifth key is having a plan). These are important enough to list again:

- *Physical exercise,* ideally every day.
- *Mental challenge* involving new learning and complex problems to solve.
- *Social connection* with friends, family, and community.
- *Passion,* a challenging pursuit you care about.

Let yourself go as you generate your list of options. Don't cross anything out. Don't censor! Go out of your way to include fanciful things you probably won't actually do. We encourage you to be a bit wild and crazy.

And make this a *long* list of options—try for at least fifty possibilities. You can evaluate and select later. You might need several brainstorming sessions to get to fifty items. If you put your list aside and come back to it later, you might be surprised at the new things you think of.

As you start brainstorming, consider what might put you in a creative, relaxed mood. For instance, play your favorite CD, light some aromatic candles, and relax with a glass of wine and some cheese. Or, if nature relaxes you, do this activity while sitting in your Jacuzzi with some close friends. Why not?!

Add Five More Options

We've found from experience that the last few ideas in brainstorming often emerge as winners. Take a few minutes and review your list. Now add five more options. While you may not act on these options later, some say that their best ideas for their New Phases came from this last quick session!

TWO MORE CREATIVE TOOLS FOR DEVISING OPTIONS

In our research and talking with individuals like you, we have discovered two creative tools helpful in reconnecting with lost memories and dreams. Use these to help to trigger even more options for your Next Phase.

Creative Tool #1: Collage

Collage is a free-form assembly or display of images and materials on any surface that creates a new whole. As you assemble your picture or image collage on a poster board, please have fun while you tap into forgotten memories and new dreams.

You'll need a large, clear work surface with plenty of light and comfortable seating. Gather the following materials to put into your collage: old magazines, catalogs, copies of photos you have taken (photocopies are okay), newspapers, and old photographs that did not make it into the albums. You'll also need: scissors, glue, tape, and two large pieces of poster board (the extra is for upsizing or a revised version).

Go through the magazines, catalogs, and newspapers and cut out images and pictures that appeal to you and could possibly represent your future. After you have cut out fifteen to twenty images and pictures, arrange these onto the poster board. Glue, tape, or paste them in place.

After you complete your collage, if you are Outgoing show it to your spouse or friends and tell about it. Take notes as you talk about the memories and dreams and learn from the inspiration. If you have a Contemplative Social Style, make some notes about your collage and then show it to your spouse or a close friend and tell about it. Take notes.

"I'll be forty on my sixtieth birthday."

CHARLES'S COLLAGE

While Charles pondered the question "what about retiring?" he took action. Remember his plan to attend the county employees' retirement workshop? He went. In an e-mail to his son afterward, Charles told about it.

> *Peter,*
>
> *Hope you are well! I just got back from the retirement workshop. The leader had us make a collage of our childhood. I got right into it. You know I enjoy doing things with my hands. I cut*

out pictures from old magazines and pasted them on a poster board. One was a picture of two kids with a lemonade stand. It reminded me of a summer when I was a child. My talkative buddy, Jake, wanted to sell lemonade to make money. I scouted the streets, went to various intersections, and counted the passing traffic. I even counted the numbers of cars that slowed down. Jake and I then picked the site for our stand and stood there to find the best time to sell—when the factory let out for lunch. On the first day, while Jake flagged down the cars, I poured the lemonade and took the money—a lot of it! Great memory.

Went home from the workshop, dug up an old phone number I had for Jake, and called it. He answered! After all these years. Had a great talk about old times. He actually complimented me on the great marketing plan I had for selling lemonade that summer—and asked if I'd ever thought of working in marketing research.

Get this: Jake offered me a job! I'll tell you more when you get here next weekend, but I feel like some doors are opening for my retirement—and I'm pretty excited.

Love,
Dad

Sometimes a small thing, like Charles's memory of the lemonade stand, is all it takes to trigger an exciting option such as the one Charles found. Later that night Charles added the following new options to his list:

- Take a full-time job in Jake's company
- Retire part-time and work part-time for Jake as a marketing consultant
- Go back to school and take some marketing courses
- Get a job at market research firm

The next morning when Charles went online, he found an e-mail from Peter:

> *Dad,*
>   *This sounds great! But maybe you should add to your option list to ". . . take a six-month leave from county job to consider what's next . . ."*
> *Love,*
Peter

Charles smiled and thought, "Yes, maybe I should . . ."

Creative Tool #2: Lifeline

While a collage is extremely helpful to many of our clients and seminar attendees, the second creative tool, lifeline, is equally inspiring and can also trigger many creative ideas. With the lifeline, you will fill in personal "highs" and "lows" over the decades, including the future. The goal of doing this exercise is to find new or newly remembered ideas for the future, inspired by past events or predicted major life events.

You can copy the lifeline (page 130) on a poster board or use the diagram in the book.

Start with specific events in your life. On the lifeline make a large dot for each event and label each dot. For instance, Pamela graduated from college in 1973, so she marked that date on her lifeline and labeled it. Consider adding high points like graduations from high school and college, weddings, first full-time job, first big career achievement, and first child born. Now the challenge: put high points in the future—years that have not happened, 2010, 2015, 2020, and so on. Some you might consider: a Mediterranean cruise, a business venture, building a new house, running a marathon, starting an art project, or getting a degree. Look forward to events you hope to enjoy someday. Share the lifeline with

Lifeline

World Events   *My Life*

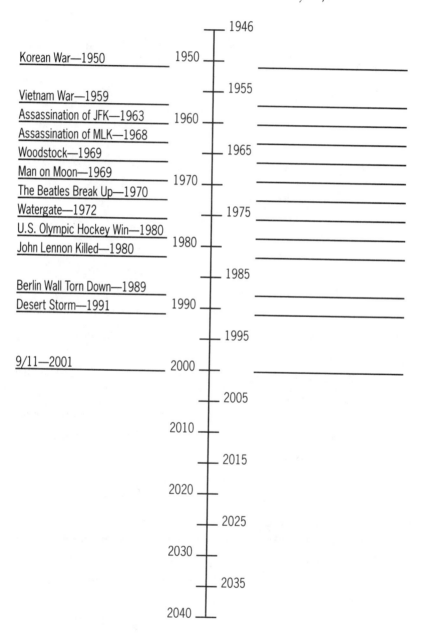

your spouse or close friend and take notes about the memories and dreams it inspires.

We hope you enjoyed the creative activities in this chapter—and that they helped free your mind to think in ways you don't ordinarily think. As you brainstormed possible options for your future, we hope you had some nice surprises.

If you're ready to select options to pursue, turn to chapter 8 to learn more about your personality and choices for the future. We'll help you determine whether you are Cautious or Optimistic, and explain how this key personality trait influences the way you narrow your options for your Next Phase. We'll give you some easy ways to reduce your list to the most attractive choices for your best retirement.

CHAPTER 8

What Is Your Outlook Style?

How Understanding Your Outlook Style Will Help You
Select the Ingredients of Your Next Phase

"I knew I could find plenty of good options for retirement if I tried. But I came up with so many. As a lifelong optimist, though, I have to question my first impulses. I've learned I often don't see the potential problems at first. I have to look again and see past my optimism."

Pamela, age fifty-five

"After years of raising kids and managing the household, I'm excited about discovering new possibilities for my future. Sometimes I have a tendency to be too optimistic, so I need to carefully assess those options that are most appealing and then talk with my husband and sisters to see if they'll really work for me."

Laura, age fifty-five

"My girlfriend Colleen sometimes calls me a pessimist. I tell her I'm a realist. I often see problems that she misses. I believe that if you anticipate trouble, you can take measures to prevent it."

Charles, age fifty-seven

PAMELA, LAURA, AND CHARLES ALL LEARNED ABOUT THEMSELVES as they progressed through the self-awareness tasks and planning steps of the My Next Phase process. Each had brainstormed a list of options, as we hope you did. (If you haven't yet created your own list, please consider going back to page 122 and following the instructions.) In this chapter we'll show you how to narrow that list by selecting the Best Options for your personality and circumstances. At the end of this chapter, you'll have all the ingredients of your Next Phase.

HOW CAUTIOUS VS. OPTIMISTIC OUTLOOK STYLES INFLUENCE CHOICES ABOUT OPTIONS

As you prepare to narrow your list of options, your Outlook Style will influence the way you tend to evaluate your choices—with optimism, caution, or with a balance between the two. Becoming aware of your Outlook Style can help you temper your optimism so you don't underestimate the risks, or rein in your caution so you don't underestimate the benefits. If you're mindful of your Outlook Style (see next page), you can realistically evaluate options.

For example, people with strongly Optimistic outlooks may barge ahead without fully investigating problems they can anticipate. Remember Ron's Optimistic yet shortsighted decision to retire to the golf course (chapter 1)? He left his optimism unchecked in planning his retirement. Though he knew better (we think!), he did not anticipate possible problems, such as no one to play golf with him.

Let's revisit Pamela and Charles from chapter 7. Their experiences in creating their list of options illustrate how individual Outlook Style can influence choices about the future. First consider Pamela, the burned-out nurse.

Pamela's Dilemma: Too Many Attractive Choices

An optimist, Pamela eagerly considered the options on her list—until she began to feel overwhelmed with the many attractive choices. "I certainly can't do all of these," she told her friend Wanda. "But they all look so appealing. How can I narrow down the choices to a few that fit best?"

PERSONALITY QUIZ #5: WHAT IS YOUR OUTLOOK STYLE? CAUTIOUS VS. OPTIMISTIC

Consider how you think, feel, and act *most of the time* when away from work and free to be yourself. Mark each statement *true* or *false*. If a statement is sometimes true and other times false, mark it *true* if it describes you even *slightly* more often than not. Avoid responses based on your work role or what others expect or how you'd like to be. If in doubt, go with your *first reaction* or *intuition*.

True   **False**

❏   ❏   1. My friends say I usually find a way to see the glass as half empty.

❏   ❏   2. When evaluating a new venture, I notice the problems and risks right away.

❏   ❏   3. My motto: "Better safe than sorry."

❏   ❏   4. If something can go wrong, it usually will.

❏   ❏   5. Trusting somebody too soon will generally invite trouble.

❏   ❏   6. Often I have to point out the risks and hazards that others miss.

❏   ❏   7. I have such a sharp eye for problems, I can see them before they happen.

❏   ❏   8. An ounce of prevention really is worth a pound of cure.

❏   ❏   9. I believe that dreams are like rainbows: only fools chase them.

❏   ❏   10. Friends count on me to pay attention to the downside.

_____ My total score (count the number of boxes marked *true*)

What Your Score Means

A score of 7, 8, 9, or 10 indicates a Cautious Outlook Style—the higher the score, the more consistent your preference for this style. A score of 4, 5, or 6 indicates a Mixed Cautious/Optimistic Outlook Style. A score of 0, 1, 2, or 3 shows an Optimistic Outlook Style—the lower the score, the more consistent your preference for an Optimistic Outlook

Cautious Outlook Style (7–10): Attuned to possible difficulties, you watch out for problems and approach life with a healthy skepticism—even pessimism. You tend to believe that whatever can go wrong, will go wrong. You stay vigilant, anticipate trouble, and do what you can to prevent it. Sometimes you expect the worst and, therefore, do not risk committing yourself. You might aim too low when setting goals. At times you prepare for the worst and go ahead. Other times, you might anticipate a problem before it exists, and perhaps bypass an opportunity out of overcaution.

Mixed Cautious/Optimistic Outlook Style (4–6): Your personality combines Cautious and Optimistic outlooks about equally. In some situations you expect problems and watch out for trouble, and in other situations, you look on the bright side and expect good results. Often in evaluating your options you can see both the probable risks and the potential benefits. You may experience ambivalence, as you can easily envision both best-case and worst-case scenarios. Your ambivalence might sometimes make it difficult for you to proceed, and at other times your realism allows you to move forward with confidence.

Optimistic Outlook Style (0–3): Generally confident of success, you expect things to go well, and you assume you can solve problems that arise. You tend to envision a bright future, and usually believe that whatever can go right, eventually will. You ordinarily don't like to think about problems that might arise, preferring to deal with them when and if they do. Your high expectations can become self-fulfilling prophecies. However, you may overlook predictable sources of trouble or underestimate risks.

Your Personality Profile

Record your Outlook Style (Cautious, Mixed, or Optimistic) on the Personality Profile module below. Then turn to the last chapter in the book, where you'll find your Personality Profile showing all seven traits (page 185). Record the result for your Outlook Style there, too, to review later. You should have five of seven traits recorded on your profile now.

My Outlook Style

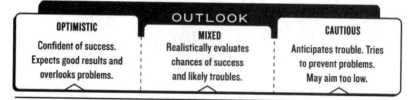

OPTIMISTIC	OUTLOOK MIXED	CAUTIOUS
Confident of success. Expects good results and overlooks problems.	Realistically evaluates chances of success and likely troubles.	Anticipates trouble. Tries to prevent problems. May aim too low.

Pamela's Optimistic Outlook Style combined with her Visionary Information Style to lead her to see positive potential in the choices before her. With her big-picture style of perceiving, she easily envisioned possibilities for the future, yet had to work at seeing practical, day-to-day details. With her Optimistic Outlook Style, she immediately saw the bright side of any situation, yet tended to overlook the dark side. So when she read her long list of options, she naturally felt like a kid in a candy shop!

Expectation of success (Optimistic Outlook Style) plus difficulty attending to practical details (Visionary Information Style) can create a recipe for disappointment. For example, when Pamela took the job of nursing supervisor, anticipating success in serving the many patients of the Pediatric Department, she discovered too late the obstacles to realizing her rosy vision of the future.

During a vacation with Wanda, Pamela enjoyed a drink after dinner as the two friends chatted about their experiences over the past thirty years. Wanda remarked on Pamela's gift for seeing the good in life, and suggested Pamela apply that gift to choosing her Best Options. "Pamela, pretend your list is a horse race, and the options are horses. Pick the ones you want to win."

Pamela instantly agreed. "What a good idea!" She went through her list and started putting stars next to her winners. She soon had stars by more than half of them. "Okay, I narrowed down the list a little, but it looks like my horse race ends in a huge tie," she said.

Wanda then suggested, "Try giving yourself three stars to put by the horses you'd bet on, or maybe dollar signs. First let's talk about your winners so far. I want to hear what you like about each one, and then let's see if you can get down to three."

Conversation continued into the night, and winners emerged. Pamela chose three "finalists," as she called them. One, in particular, began to stand out: the possibility of going to divinity school and getting ordained as a minister.

Through our experience in coaching people through the process of planning for retirement, we've found it most effective to select options that look best, as Pamela did. After picking your winners, you can explore further. Natural Optimists, like Pamela, readily see the prospects for success and later have to work at seeing the problems. In contrast, those with strongly Cautious Outlook Styles easily see problems—and may be tempted to start eliminating losers right away. We strongly advise against that! Instead, we suggest that they put off thinking about problems for a while, keep an open mind, and focus on the appeal of each option. Usually they can identify the most attractive prospects—as we hope you will.

Pamela's Options—Partial List

- Help house the homeless
- Open a soup kitchen for the homeless at my church
- Become a pediatric nurse at Toronto General Hospital with Wanda
- Become a navy medic with Julie
- Become a foster parent for HIV newborns
- Become a public-health nurse at an elementary school
- Work in a private pediatric practice
- Organize a Bible study group at church
- Senior rowing team
- Marathon training with Betty and Vivian
- Camping with Wanda
- Nurse at a hospital in England or Europe
- Give powerful speeches on human rights to packed auditoriums
- Lead a parade of like-minded individuals in an effort to conquer poverty
- Work at a medical spa in California
- Practice massage therapy
- Wallpaper and redo the lower level
- Go to divinity school and become an ordained Unitarian minister
- Work with Alzheimer's patients at an adult daycare
- Do health-care house calls for the elderly
- Organize a vegetarian diet group at church
- Formulate a spiritual development plan in consultation with a mentor at the Unitarian Universalist Association
- Bridge with Katherine, Sarah, and Rafael
- Plan an annual family reunion—parents, brothers, their families—at a beach resort

Charles's Question Revisited

Remember Charles, the statistician for a county government we introduced in the last chapter? He received an e-mail from his son, Peter, asking, *"What about retiring?"* Weeks later that question lingered in Charles's mind.

Charles has a Cautious Outlook Style, just the opposite of Pamela's. Charles tends to expect trouble and see the pitfalls ahead. Sensitivity to risks makes it difficult for him to consider unfamiliar options. Once he identifies a hazard of a particular course of action, however unlikely it seems to others, he begins to shy away and perhaps dismiss it.

"It's my nature, I guess," Charles said. "I focus on the risks and problems—and sometimes immediately reject suggestions my girlfriend, Colleen, sees as quite feasible."

Charles's Cautious Outlook Style combined with his Practical Information Style drives his attention to the specific defects in the options he considers. With his detail-oriented (Practical) style of perceiving the world, Charles sees the specifics of any option. He feels comfortable with known or familiar alternatives but is suspicious of unproven ones. With his Cautious Outlook Style, Charles looks first to practical details that could cause trouble. He often says, "Yes, but what if . . ." and points out a pitfall that could derail a plan—especially an untried one. Charles quickly sees the small defects and all too easily overlooks larger benefits. And, like many with a Cautious Outlook Style, he overestimates the probability of something actually going wrong. So when Charles reread his list of options, he zeroed in on the problems and saw them looming large.

Focus on procedural details (Practical Information Style) plus a tendency to expect the worst (Cautious Outlook Style) can lead to bypassing opportunities. For example, Charles had a job offer from his old friend Jake that would take him into a pursuit completely unfamiliar to him—marketing research. Of course Charles thought of obstacles that might trip him up if he chose that option, and it began to slide toward the bottom of his list.

In brainstorming possibilities for his Next Phase, Charles listed concrete, specific options. As you would expect for someone with a Practical Information Style, Charles felt most comfortable with familiar alternatives, so he listed particular places he knew, actions he could take, and time frames he understood. Notice that his list below names the locations and times, such as the university he would consider attending for a PhD in statistics. (Compare Pamela's list, reflecting her Visionary Information Style, which leaves most such details unspecified.) In addition, as you would expect for someone with a Contemplative Social Style, Charles listed pursuits that involved one-to-one relationships, activities with one other person, and solitary pursuits, and few activities involving groups.

Charles wrote Peter an e-mail to keep him updated:

Peter,

I'm seriously considering several options for my future. But you know me. The more I think about each option, the more risks I begin to notice. The only secure option I see right now is to continue working for the county for another decade. At least I already know the problems.

Maybe I need a second opinion. What do you think?

Love,

Dad

Like so many with a Cautious Outlook Style, Charles benefits from exploring and understanding options before dismissing them as too risky. We find it most effective for those who are Cautious to first identify options that look like a good fit. After selecting the winners, they can review the problems—and, ideally, get other viewpoints to help them see positive possibilities as clearly as potential pitfalls. Getting a second opinion can also help someone with a

Cautious Outlook Style more realistically estimate the chances of something going wrong. This puts the fear of failure into perspective, and makes it easier to focus on the benefits of success.

Charles's Options—Expanded List
(*items added when he expanded the list*)

- Get a PhD from the statistics program at Ohio State University
- Ask Colleen to marry me at the end of the year
- Move to Phoenix and work full-time as a statistician for the state of Arizona
- Take evening classes in marketing at Ohio State
- Take the job in Mick's company as a statistician
- Take a job in marketing research in Jake's company
- Retire and work 40 percent time for Jake as a marketing research consultant
- *Join YMCA neighborhood fitness center and start an exercise program
- *Purchase a treadmill—Colleen
- *Volunteer to organize the inventory at the Mid-Ohio Food Bank
- *Take Pete to Vancouver for spawning of the whales in March
- *Finish the basement and make two offices
- *Serve on the finance committee at church
- *Lose ten pounds by the end of the year
- *Take swing dancing lessons with Colleen at Swing Columbus
- * Look for a Catholic church to join
- *Get season tickets for the Columbus Symphony Orchestra
- *Join the Columbus Museum of Art

NARROW YOUR LIST OF OPTIONS

Now that you have determined your Outlook Style, go back to your list of options. It's time to start narrowing down your options to select the ones that fit best for you. Follow these five steps:

> *Step 1*: Consider your Outlook Style (Cautious vs. Optimistic) and adopt a fitting mind-set
>
> *Step 2*: Grade the options on your list as "okay," "better," or "best"
>
> *Step 3*: Create your List of Best Options
>
> *Step 4*: Ask two friends about your List of Best Options
>
> *Step 5*: Screen your List of Best Options for your Next Phase

Step 1: Consider Your Outlook Style and Adopt a Fitting Mind-set

Depending on your Outlook Style, we'd like you to adopt one of the following three mind-sets in selecting and reviewing your Best Options:

1. OPTIMISTIC OUTLOOK STYLE

If you have an Optimistic Outlook Style, select your favorite options without regard for their feasibility. Realize that you'll tend to miss problems at first, so start now to identify backup options to consider when you eventually have to eliminate some of your favorites. Prepare to get help seeing the risks by asking two close friends to discuss them with you.

2. CAUTIOUS OUTLOOK STYLE

If you take a Cautious Outlook, select your favorite options and briefly note the biggest problems or risks you see. This should be easy for you. For now, ignore the problems you have noted and focus on what you like about every option on your list. Don't cross out or dismiss any options yet. Realize that you might overlook possible benefits or quit trying to find ways to make the option work. Please suspend judgment—just for a while—and prepare to get help seeing the benefits by asking two close friends to discuss them with you.

3. MIXED OUTLOOK STYLE

Select those options that appeal most to you. You can review these and *do a risk-benefit analysis later, not now.* Meanwhile prepare to get confirmation of your risk-benefit analysis by asking two close friends to discuss it with you.

Step 2: Grade the Options

Now it's time to review your list and mark each option on the list for one of three groups. To make it quick and easy, give each option a grade such as A (best), B (better), or C (okay), as follows:

1. Best Options (your favorites)   A
2. Better Options (good choices but not the best)   B
3. Okay Options (so-so or fair)   C

Please aim for about a dozen Best Options (A), but don't worry if you come up with more or fewer.

A word of advice: don't edit, rearrange, combine, or delete any options from your long list now! Don't classify or categorize. Don't do anything to your list except add more items. Then pick your favorites. Over the years we've seen many people waste time trying to reduce their original lists by categorizing at this stage. That just makes the options more difficult to see. Leave the list as it is, and choose from what's there. If something is missing, add it. If something needs rephrasing, add the rephrased version.

Step 3: Create Your List of Best Options

On a separate page, go ahead and rewrite your Best Options (those graded A) to make a short list. Start with the options that appeal the most to you—regardless of potential problems. Focus on what attracts you.

Once you've written your short list of Best Options, read the original list of options again. Do you see options on the long list that you want to claim? Add them now to the new short list of Best Options. (Don't worry about having too many options on your short list. You can narrow it later, after talking with friends.)

Step 4: Ask Two Friends about Your List of Best Options

Now it's time to follow up and get that second opinion. Once you have identified your Best Options, we strongly suggest that you show your list to at least two close friends (one at a time if you are Contemplative). What you ask of them depends on your Outlook Style:

1. OPTIMISTIC OUTLOOK STYLE

Ask your friends to look at your list of Best Options and point out the potential *problems*. Do not argue or defend! Just listen to their cautions with an ear to hearing how you may have overreached or headed unknowingly into a minefield.

After considering your friends' input, you can more realistically assess the Best Options on your list, taking into consideration the problems and risks they pointed out. For now, please stretch a bit: focus on the problems. See the roadblocks—not the possibilities! *Get in touch with your inner pessimist!* And prepare to run several sets of options past your friends.

2. CAUTIOUS OUTLOOK STYLE

Ask your friends to look at your list of Best Options and point out the *benefits* and to estimate the probability of the problems you have identified. Do not argue with them or defend! Just listen with an ear to hearing how you may have underestimated yourself or your chances of success by focusing too much on problems.

After considering your friends' input, you can more realistically assess the Best Options on your list, taking into consideration the benefits they pointed out and their estimates of success. For now, please stretch a bit and focus on success. See the possibilities—not the roadblocks. *Get in touch with your inner optimist!* And prepare to revise downward your estimates of the probability that something will go wrong.

3. MIXED (REALISTIC) OUTLOOK STYLE

Summarize your risk-benefit analysis for each option and ask your friends how realistic each seems to them. Do not argue or defend! Just listen to their views of the risks and benefits, with an ear to hearing how you may have over- or underemphasized something. After considering your friends' input, reassess the Best Options on your list, taking into consideration their estimates of the risks and benefits.

Step 5: Screen Your List of Best Options for Your Next Phase

If your list of Best Options is like others in our seminars and coaching sessions, it needs fine-tuning. The most effective way we've found involves screening it against the points listed below. They incorporate the five keys to successful retirement we mentioned earlier. Review your list against the screening points, one at a time. If you see that your Best Options include what's needed, put a check mark in the space. One option can satisfy more than one screening point. For instance, swing dancing is both exercise and fun. If you see something missing from your Best Options, add new items to your list, then check off that screening point.

Review the ten points again. Do you see any unchecked? If so, add the missing options. Remember to take your revised list back to your friends for the Outlook Style check.

One more word of advice: many lists include options that won't work well for specific reasons and need rethinking. For example, if your Best Option for physical activity is skiing and you live in Alabama, you'll get exercise for only two weeks out of the year! Cross off any obvious misfits on your list.

TEN WAYS TO SCREEN YOUR BEST OPTIONS

#1: *Physical Exercise* _____

As we've noted several times, regular physical exercise promotes health, quality of life, and longevity as we age, so it is essential to your future. We've talked with hundreds of retired men and women. Those who stay physically active have better health, greater energy, and more satisfying retirements. As you review your list of Best Options, be sure to include some form of regular exercise.

#2: *Mental Challenge* _____

This second key to a successful Next Phase comes from pursuits involving complex problem solving and new learning. Among the many examples: learning a new language, writing for publication, playing competitive bridge or chess, taking music lessons.

#3: *Social Connection* _____

Social connection represents the third key to a successful retirement. Find a way to build regular interaction with friends (not just your mate and family members) into your life. Examples: active involvement in community and religious organizations, political activities, professional associations, teaching, etc.

#4: *Passion* _____

For this fourth key to a successful retirement—your reason to get out of bed each morning—make sure you feel passionate about something on your Best Options list.

#5: Close Relationships _____

Review the options on your list that potentially involve others to make sure they work well with those people you care about, such as your mate, friends, and family. For example, if you want to take drum lessons or learn to play the acoustic guitar, run it by your mate first. If you want to travel for months out of the year, make sure your mate agrees. Now confirm, modify, or drop Best Options on the list, depending on the responses.

#6: Work Fulfillment _____

You have a list of your main sources of fulfillment from work on page 100. Go back and review that list. Make sure the Best Options on your list bring the kind(s) of fulfillment you want to carry forward from work. As an example, if exercising influence in people's lives has given you fulfillment at work, try to include a pursuit that enables you to have influence in your new phase. Examples include babysitting grandchildren, mentoring or coaching individuals, teaching a class, or leading an organization or group.

#7: Personality Fit _____

Your personality fit includes your specific traits—including your Social, Planning, Stress, Activity, and Outlook Styles. Review your Personality Profile on page 185 and delete the options on your list incompatible with your traits. For example, someone with a Contemplative Social Style probably should not take a part-time sales job. Outgoing individuals would be bored sitting in a forest-fire watchtower. Someone with a Responsive Stress Style should not volunteer to be a scoutmaster or an Emergency Medical Services technician.

#8: Continuing Pursuits _____

As you consider your list of Best Options, include activities that you now enjoy and want to continue in your Next Phase. Examples include exercise routines, attending symphony concerts with your friends, visits with family, annual professional conferences, or writing for publication. Did you forget any? Add those you want to continue.

#9: Reality Check _____

Now review your list again and apply four reality checks. Do you have the necessary *time, money, physical capability,* and *personal support* the activity requires?

In chapter 10 we discuss reviewing your plan for your Next Phase with your financial adviser—and, if necessary, making adjustments. Many people shortchange themselves by allowing their financial situations to keep them from exploring attractive options for a new phase. In our seminars and coaching, we see a pattern: those who make plans for new phases that fit their personalities and circumstances—nonfinancial plans—usually find creative ways to make the finances work. They figure out the financing after planning what they'll do with their lives. You can, too. We also have found many financial advisers very receptive to these plans. Many breathe sighs of relief when they see specific, thoughtful plans. Now they can advise and suggest financial approaches much more easily. Your options are no longer moving targets. Of course once the options hold still, you may have to eliminate some of them, like those you truly can't afford, can't do because of physical limitations, or that get vetoed by your mate or support network.

#10: Balance Overall _____

Finally, make sure you see balance for *you* in the list of Best Options. This means balancing fun with work, social life with solitary time, home time with travel, and physical activity with rest.

Pamela's List of Best Options

- Organize a soup kitchen at my church
- Practice massage therapy
- Formulate a spiritual development plan in consultation with a mentor at the Unitarian Universalist Association
- Senior rowing team
- Marathon training with Vivian and Betty
- Learn how to wallpaper and redo the lower level
- Attend divinity school and become an ordained Unitarian minister
- Bridge with Katherine, Sarah, and Rafael
- Organize vegetarian diet group at church
- Camping with Wanda
- Work with Alzheimer's patients at adult daycare
- Annual family reunions—parents, brothers, and their families—at beach resort

Charles's List of Best Options

- Ask Colleen to marry me at the end of the year
- Take evening classes in marketing at Ohio State
- Retire and work 40 percent time for Jake as a marketing research consultant
- Exercise at YMCA neighborhood fitness center
- Morning walks with Colleen
- Volunteer office accounting at Mid-Ohio Food Bank
- Season tickets to Columbus Symphony Orchestra with Colleen, Jack, and Alice
- Take Pete to Vancouver for spawning of the whales in March
- Finish the basement and make two offices
- Volunteer to serve on the finance committee at church
- Swing dancing with Colleen at Swing Columbus
- Attend local Catholic church

"It helps supplement my Social Security."

THE INGREDIENTS OF YOUR NEXT PHASE

How will you convert your Best Options into Ingredients of your Next Phase? Choose options that represent *continuing long-term pursuits for your future* in the categories on page 153. These go beyond one-time events. Your Ingredients should consist of activities you can sustain, and involvements and commitments that will last over the years. When you look at your list of Ingredients two or three years from now, it should still guide your future.

• If you have a Visionary Information Style, like Pamela, you might see many more possibilities than you can actually pursue, even in several years. You'll have to let some go.

• If you see *unique one-time events* on your list of Best Options, convert them to long-term Ingredients by naming the continuing activities they represent. For example, Charles listed a trip with Pete to Vancouver in the spring to see the whales. Later he realized that this one-time event was part of a tradition. Charles had taken Pete on annual vacation trips since Pete was five years old, and he intended to continue. So for Charles the Ingredient became: *Annual trips with Pete; start with Vancouver in March to see whales.*

• Look for *options with a common theme* and combine them. For example, your list may include several travel destinations. If so, put the destinations together like Charles did in this new Ingredient: *Travel with Colleen to California, Washington, other western states, England, Europe.* Add the combined option to your Ingredients List.

• Now claim all or some of your Best Options as **Ingredients** *of your Next Phase.* Using the list on page 153, consider one or two of your Best Options for each and write them on the page. (See how Pamela and Charles defined their ingredients on pages 152 and 154.)

Aim for at Least One Option per Category

Before you leave a category blank on page 153, think it over. If you still don't want it, move on. For instance, some people don't want to include an option for spirituality. Others don't want to get involved with their families of origin anymore. If you're single and intend to stay that way, you don't need the mate category. Consider each category.

Some options will fit in more than one place. For example, Pamela included "Training for a marathon with Vivian and Betty" as a friendship activity and as exercise. Go ahead and list the same option in more than one place if it makes sense to do so. Don't let the categories get in your way.

After putting your Best Options into the categories, put your list aside for a while. Let it marinate. Think about and/or discuss with those close to you what you have in mind. Talk with your mate, a relative, a friend. Ask for feedback and consider the opinions.

Ingredients of Pamela's Next Phase — First Draft

- *Health/Exercise* — Marathon training with Vivian and Betty; senior rowing team; organize vegetarian diet group at church
- *Challenging Pursuit* — Attend divinity school and become ordained as a Unitarian minister; marathon training with Vivian and Betty
- *Relationship with Mate/Life Partner* — None
- *Friendship* — Camping with Wanda; marathon training with Vivian and Betty; bridge with Katherine, Sarah, and Rafael
- *Family* — Annual family reunions with parents, brothers, and their families at beach resort
- *Self-Development/Spirituality* — Attend theology school; formulate a spiritual development plan in consultation with a mentor at the Unitarian Universalist Association
- *Fun/Enjoyment* — Bridge with Katherine, Sarah, and Rafael; marathon training with Vivian and Betty; practice massage therapy
- *Home/House/Residence* — Home renovation projects: start with wallpapering and redoing lower level
- *Community* — Neighborhood Homeless Outreach Committee; organize soup kitchen at church; work with Alzheimer's patients at adult daycare
- *Other* — None

Ingredients of Charles's Next Phase — First Draft

- *Health/Exercise* — Work out daily at neighborhood Y
- *Challenging Pursuit* — Work 40 percent time as marketing consultant in Jake's firm
- *Relationship with Mate/Life Partner* – Ask Colleen to marry me at the end of the year
- *Friendship* — Season tickets for Columbus Symphony Orchestra with Colleen, Jack, and Alice; work out daily at the Y; take evening classes in marketing at Ohio State

Ingredients of My Next Phase

• Health/Exercise _____

• _____

• Challenging Pursuit _____

• _____

• Relationship with Mate/Life Partner _____

• _____

• Friendship _____

• _____

• Family _____

• _____

• Self-Development/Spirituality _____

• _____

• Fun/Enjoyment _____

• _____

• Home/House/Residence _____

• _____

• Community _____

• _____

• Other _____

- *Family*—Annual trips with Pete; start with Vancouver in March to see whales
- *Self-Development/Spirituality*–Attend local Catholic church
- *Fun/Enjoyment*—Swing dancing at Swing Columbus with Colleen; season tickets for Columbus Symphony Orchestra with Colleen, Jack, and Alice
- *Home/House/Residence*—Finish basement and set up two offices
- *Community*—Volunteer at Mid-Ohio Food Bank
- *Other*—Travel with Colleen to California, Washington, other western states, England, Europe

NAME YOUR NEXT PHASE

Through our years of coaching boomers as they plan for the future, we've found it helpful to give the new phase a name. Ideally the name concisely captures the essence, theme, vision, or thrust of what's next. It often energizes planning and decision making. Having a name for your Next Phase can help you see additional possibilities later. If you know what you're looking for, you just might find it!

The name you give your Next Phase gives you an answer to the question you'll get at parties and social gatherings: "What are you doing these days?" Saying "I'm retired" tends to be a conversation stopper. In contrast, many of our clients have discovered that merely mentioning the names of their new phases can open dialogues, help connect with others, make new contacts, and aid in networking. As an example, Pamela named her Next Phase "UUMMinistry," which proved to be a conversation starter for her. Charles named his future "Swinging Stats Consultant" (in case you missed it, he had swing dancing with Colleen on his list of ingredients). Here are some examples of names from www.MyNext Phase.com.

Second Career

Downshift

Calling

Passion

Adventure Travel

Lakeside Retreat

Un-retirement

Retreat

Bliss

Rewired/Rewiring

Downsizing

Resizing

Urban Adventure

Mountain

Exploration

Simplifying

Seaside Haven

Career Light (or Lite)

Adventuring

Deepening the Roots

Keeping On

Exploring/Explorer

Living for Today

Call to Service

Volunteer

Retooling

Redeveloping

Redirecting

Pilgrimage

New Direction

Renaissance

Reinvention

Refuge

Rooting

Now take a few minutes and go over your short list of Best Options again. What name captures your vision of what you might do for the rest of your life?

YOUR PLAN IS STILL A WORK IN PROGRESS!

Up to now in this chapter, you've determined your Outlook Style, either Cautious or Optimistic (or Mixed). You created your list of Best Options and screened them using the ten criteria for successful retirement. Then you defined the Ingredients of your Next Phase, putting some of your Best Options into the categories. Finally, you gave your Next Phase a name—to bring it to life and make it more real to you and others.

In this last part of the chapter, please spend a few minutes to make a second draft of the Ingredients of your Next Phase. We hope that by now you've given these ingredients more thought, or even talked to your mate or best friend about them. Perhaps naming your Next Phase inspired you to change or add options.

As you revise the Ingredients, review the list of personality traits and needs below and make sure you've included the right options. For instance, Pamela's an Optimist, so she needs hope—and to balance that need she must make sure she has not overlooked potential roadblocks on the pathway to becoming a minister.

Charles is Cautious and needs security. To balance that need, he should pay attention to opportunities that stretch his zone of comfort, like the job with Jake. He probably has to fight his tendency to look for problems that would confirm his initial fears about taking the job.

Consider Your Personality Traits and Needs

Following is a list of the seven pairs of personality traits, along with key personal needs associated with each. For instance, if you have a Cautious Outlook Style, like Charles, this list shows that you feel a need for security. Take a moment to identify your own traits and needs. Try to identify your top three personal needs on this list.

Personality Traits	Felt Needs
Outgoing	Face time, people, action
Contemplative	Solitude, downtime
Responsive	Retreat, support
Resilient	Challenge, adventure
Independent	Autonomy
Interdependent	Cooperation
Practical	Traditions
Visionary	Innovation
Optimistic	Hope
Cautious	Security
Empathetic	Harmony, interpersonal comfort
Analytic	Logic, clarity

| Flexible | Unscheduled time |
| Structured | Daily routine |

As you evaluate your options for a new phase, it helps to understand your Outlook—Optimistic versus Cautious. If you consistently tend to take one of the two outlooks in many different situations, you may already be aware of your preference. Those close to you may have called it to your attention, as Peter did with Charles. Once aware of your Outlook Style, you can keep it in mind as you choose your role models for retirement (chapter 9) and set goals for your future (chapter 10).

CHAPTER 9

What Is Your Decision Style?

How to Use Your Decision Style to Choose the Best Role Models for Retirement

PETER'S INTERVIEWS

At fifty-two, Peter decided to take early retirement from his career as a marketing executive. He knew he didn't want to retire to leisure. He also knew he wanted a less demanding career—one that allowed time and freedom to pursue other interests besides work. Healthy and vital, Peter was determined to go into a new field. But what career would he choose?

After working through the My Next Phase process, Peter knew he had a Mixed Outgoing/Contemplative Social Style, which led him to career choices that mixed solitary and social pursuits. He saw that his Independent Activity Style called for autonomy.

Peter had decided that his new career would take one of three tracks, all related to travel and hospitality in Italy: freelance food-wine-travel writer, tour leader in Italy, or corporate marketing representative. However, he knew too little about these careers to make an informed decision.

To determine which path to follow, Peter planned to interview role models in all three careers. He had an extensive network from his years in marketing, with many contacts in the food, travel, and publishing industries. He made calls and scheduled interviews with the following individuals, all within three weeks:

- Ben, a senior editor for a popular food-and-wine magazine
- Magdalena, his personal travel agent and former tour guide in Italy
- Harris, a published freelance travel writer for more than twenty years
- Carlos, a marketing representative for an international hotel chain
- Charlotte, a freelance writer specializing in cultural events in Italy, Spain, and Greece

Peter asked each person a few questions about his or her life and job, and made notes in his journal. He quickly concluded that freelance writing offered the best fit for his personality. He ruled out working as a corporate marketing rep as soon as he understood that this career had limited autonomy (a must-have for his Independent Activity Style). Working as a tour leader didn't seem to offer as much creative challenge as Peter wanted.

When Peter talked at length with Harry and Charlotte, two experienced freelance writers, the conversations confirmed what he knew: he wanted to write food, wine, and travel articles for publication. Peter felt that freelance writing would give him both independence and creative challenge. Because freelance writers must promote themselves to editors and publishers, this career also tapped the knowledge and skills he had learned during his career in marketing. "The marketing connection gave me a sense of continuity. My new phase seems like a natural evolution of my career," Peter said.

Ingredients of Peter's Next Phase

- *Health/Exercise*—Daily walk, run, or gym workout for exercise. Fencing at the Studio. Hiking. Tuscan-style diet (heavy on fruits, vegetables, whole grains, fish, olive oil, red wine).
- *Challenging Pursuits*—Freelance food-travel-wine writing for media outlets and marketing and advertising firms. Italian language study.
- *Relationship with Mate*—Cooking together for other couples. Trips for two and group trips in Italy and other European countries. Hiking vacations.
- *Friendship*—Exchange home visits with three or four friends living in Italy. Collaborate with wine-writer friend, Bill. Keep up with fencing buddies from college.
- *Family*—Annual family gatherings, all four siblings and parents, in U.S. or Europe. Invite the kids to join one or two trips to Italy each year. Visit kids at their places at least once a year.
- *Self-Development*—Continued study of Italian language: private lessons, courses in Italian at college. Workshops on writing and marketing. Possibly teach courses in marketing.
- *Fun/Enjoyment*—Private tours of Italy. Wine-tasting club. Hiking. Cooking lessons in Tuscany and New York! Competitive fencing with buddies from college.
- *Home/House/Residence*—Add to collection of Italian art and sculpture.
- *Community*—Officer in Professional Food Writers' Association. Participate in condo owners group. Wine-tasting club.

WILLIAM'S REALIZATION

At sixty-two, William, a business-development executive with a large communications firm, took an enticing early-retirement package. Thinking he might find fulfillment in benevolent work, William began multiple volunteer activities, including his favorite at the city public library. While he felt that he made important contributions, William had a nagging sense of something missing from his life. When a close friend bought a new sports car, William decided to spend part of his early retirement bonus on a Porsche convertible, thinking it might lift his spirits, too.

Meanwhile, William visited www.MyNextPhase.com after talking with his friend Randy Burnham, a coauthor of this book. William took the Personality Inventory and learned about his seven traits. His profile confirmed that William had a highly Empathetic Decision Style. William naturally emphasized emotional priorities and personal relationships in his decisions, and gave less emphasis to objective achievements like money and possessions. He also learned from his Fulfillment Quiz that he gained personal fulfillment from social connections and community life. So why would William spend a huge chunk of change on a fancy sports car? According to his Personality Inventory, that type of purchase had nothing to do with his main sources of fulfillment. William realized that he had made that choice from his least-preferred decision mode—Analytic—and ignored what was most important to him. With just a little coaching, he switched to his preferred mode for making decisions—Empathetic—and quickly recognized his priorities. With self-insight, William canceled the order he'd placed for the new luxury car.

"I overestimated the importance of the comforts and luxuries that I thought I wanted," William said. "While initially the idea of owning a Porsche convertible excited me, now I find the idea a bit extravagant. I'm quite surprised! I discovered that it's more important to me to donate that money to the library where I volunteer, and I feel good about doing this."

Before we discuss the steps in deciding on role models, here is the quiz on Decision Style (next page).

PERSONALITY QUIZ #6: WHAT IS YOUR DECISION STYLE? EMPATHETIC VS. ANALYTIC

Consider how you think, feel, and act *most of the time* when away from work and free to be yourself. Mark each statement *true* or *false*. If a statement is sometimes true and other times false, mark it *true* if it describes you even *slightly* more often than not. Avoid responses based on your work role or what others expect or how you'd like to be. If in doubt, go with your *first reaction* or *intuition*.

True **False**

❏ ❏ 1. If faced with a change, I look first at the financial impact, then at the emotional side.

❏ ❏ 2. When a close friend has a problem, I try to offer the most logical solution.

❏ ❏ 3. People count on me to keep them focused on the bottom line.

❏ ❏ 4. I take pride in having others think of me as reasonable.

❏ ❏ 5. I have trouble empathizing with people who cry easily.

❏ ❏ 6. In upsetting situations I try to stay tough minded.

❏ ❏ 7. The most important thing in making a decision is the objective facts.

❏ ❏ 8. I tend to prefer the clarity of physics to the fuzziness of sociology.

❏ ❏ 9. I wish I understood relationships as well as I understand spreadsheets.

❏ ❏ 10. Call me cold and uncaring if you have to, but at least I'm logical.

_____ My total score (count the number of boxes marked *true*)

What Your Score Means

A score of 7, 8, 9, or 10 indicates an Analytic Decision Style—the higher the score, the more consistent your preference for this style. *A score of 4, 5, or 6 indicates a Mixed Analytic/Empathetic Decision Style. A score of 0, 1, 2, or 3 shows an Empathetic Decision Style*—the lower the score, the more consistent your preference for an Empathetic Style.

Analytic Decision Style (7–10): You focus on data and try to objectively analyze outcomes and costs. Dispassionate and tough minded, you prefer to make rational decisions based more on logical analysis and expected results than on feelings and emotions. Faced with change, you rely on your cool-headed logic to make your decisions.

Mixed Empathetic/Analytic Decision Style (4–6): Equally comfortable with subjective feelings and objective realities in making decisions, you can take a sympathetic or a dispassionate approach, as the situation requires. Sensitive to emotions as well as objective realities, you seek balance. At times perhaps ambivalent, you might vacillate between data and feelings and feel conflicted or confused.

Empathetic Decision Style (0–3): You focus on people's feelings, concerns, and relationships. Sympathetic and considerate, you strive to make decisions that take account of others' emotions and sensitivities. You try to stay in touch with your feelings and those of others. When faced with change, you tend to rely on your deeply felt value of relationships to shape your decisions, and trust your compassion and empathy.

> **Your Personality Profile**
>
> Record your Decision Style (Analytic, Mixed, or Empathetic) on the Personality Profile module below and add it to your Personality Profile (page 185). This gives you six of seven traits in the Profile.

My Decision Style

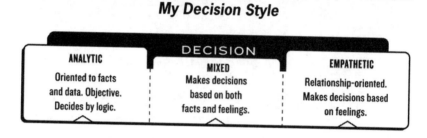

ANALYTIC	DECISION MIXED	EMPATHETIC
Oriented to facts and data. Objective. Decides by logic.	Makes decisions based on both facts and feelings.	Relationship-oriented. Makes decisions based on feelings.

When you named your Next Phase and listed its Ingredients, you began the last stage of preparation for your future: *redefining your role*. In this chapter we'll explain how to use your preferred style of decision making in selecting your role models for retirement: the people you trust to guide your decisions about the future. Like so many other decisions about retirement, your choices concerning role models reflect your unique circumstances and personality. The individuals you choose as role models or as examples of success will depend on where you need the most guidance from someone who's gone ahead of you on the path you've chosen, or can help you choose a path.

HOW DO YOU MAKE DECISIONS?

Did you gain insight into your Decision Style from taking the quiz? Understanding it can help you avoid potential roadblocks during your transition. The differences become clearer in the analogy of two favorite characters from *The Wizard of Oz:* Tin Man (head) and Scarecrow (heart).

Tin Man—Analytic Decision Style

If you have an Analytic Decision Style, like the Tin Man (head), you prefer to make decisions based on logic and objective facts. Laura, the homemaker with the empty nest (page 30), exemplifies this style. She used it in deciding on new pursuits to supplement her shrinking role of homemaker. She logically reviewed the facts of her situation—home alone with children away at college and her husband traveling on business—then made the decision.

When you overemphasize a preference for logical analysis, you can head straight into a blind spot. If you rely too much on logic, people around you will notice your lack of empathy. Applying a tough-minded style to relationships can easily discount people's feelings.

Ron, the production manager in chapter 1, illustrates how someone with an Analytic Decision Style made a decision out of an emotional blind spot. Ron talked with his wife about retiring only after making the decision with his boss. He even ignored his wife's objections! Later Ron regretted his failure to consider her feelings, along with his failure to consider his own feelings about leaving his life's work.

Scarecrow—Empathetic Decision Style

If you have an Empathetic Decision Style, like the Scarecrow (heart), you prefer to make decisions based on feelings and relationships.

Pamela, the pediatric nurse, exemplifies this style. When she decided to start her career in nursing, Pamela put helping others at the center of her life. For many years she found fulfillment from serving her patients.

Later Pamela demonstrated how someone with an Empathetic Decision Style can make a decision out of an emotional blind spot. Pamela accepted the promotion to nursing supervisor in hopes of serving even more patients (her Empathetic motive for taking the job). She skipped the logical step of talking with other supervisors about the patient load, patient-to-staff ratio, turnover rate, hiring success rates, and other questions that would have seemed natural for someone with an Analytic Decision Style. Instead, Pamela made a heartfelt decision that took her into a frustrating job that ultimately left her exhausted and burned out.

Whether you favor the Scarecrow's approach, the Tin Man's approach, or a combination (Mixed), your Decision Style will influence your choice of role models for retirement. If you follow the Scarecrow (heart) style, you'll seek a role model you like and can identify with. If you follow the Tin Man (head) style, you'll tend to look for a record of successful results.

SIX KINDS OF ROLE MODELS

As Peter discovered at the beginning of the chapter, finding the right role models to guide your Next Phase requires some thought and care . . . but it can be the key to creating a fulfilling retirement.

A role model is an individual you choose to imitate in some sphere of your own life—from a very narrow, specific skill to a whole lifestyle—or someone from whom you seek guidance. A conversation may not be possible—for instance, if you chose Winston Churchill (no longer living) or Oprah (not very accessible). If you do have a personal relationship, it might consist of a single brief interview or a longer connection.

Here are the six types of role models we've identified. Which will you seek?

1. Trailblazer

Trailblazers offer expert advice from personal experience along a path you are considering. They have firsthand knowledge of the terrain and can offer hints and warnings. For example, Peter interviewed two freelance writers about their careers in writing for food, wine, and travel magazines. He also attended seminars for travel writers, freelance food-and-wine writers, and authors, where the instructors served as trailblazers.

2. Mentor

A mentor is an experienced exemplar who volunteers extended individual guidance in a long-term personal relationship. Typically older and wiser, a mentor makes a commitment to guide your development, often through a continuing relationship like a family tie or shared membership in an organization. A mentor resembles a trailblazer who takes a personal interest. For example, Warren, fifty-eight, CEO of a small plastics fabrication business who is considering retirement, must sell his business or find a successor to run it. Thinking that a mentor might help him sort through his options, Warren remembered James, the older CEO of a competitor business whom he had befriended in an earlier patent dispute. Warren asked James if he would help him figure out how to sell or merge the business. James served as a mentor to Warren through the difficult process.

3. Teacher

A teacher specializes in helping people learn. You might say that a teacher offers secondhand knowledge, while a trailblazer offers firsthand experience. A teacher can give a good overview of the questions, and the trailblazer can offer practical, specific answers—if you know the questions. (Because those who practice a specialty don't necessarily learn how to teach it, you'll have to know what to ask.)

4. Professional Coach/Counselor

Many retirees turn to professional coaches or counselors. A coach is essentially a paid mentor, an expert who provides expert individualized guidance on a particular topic, like retirement or skiing. A counselor offers more general guidance. (Like many other organizations, www.MyNextPhase.com offers individual coaching

"The best year of your life is ahead of you."

to those considering retirement.) Professional coaching can help you expand your list of options in your career—and in the rest of your life.

5. Hero

Sometimes a role model is a hero. This is someone (living or deceased) in the media, whether from the news, on television, in biographies, or in movies or history books. Some examples might be journalist and commentator Daniel Schorr, international peacemaker and former president Jimmy Carter, Helen Keller, Winston Churchill, Mother Teresa, and others. Who is your hero? Would this person also make a positive role model for some Ingredient of your Next Phase?

6. Adviser and Sounding Board

An adviser is someone who lives closer to home. It's natural to look to those individuals closest to you for advice or to serve as a sounding board. Choose a good listener who knows you well and has your best interests at heart. You've known these people for a long time and trust them to help you with day-to-day decisions. Examples may include:

Your mate. Who knows you better than your spouse or life partner? Remember Mark, the marketing executive who failed his first try at retirement by moving to an isolated lakeside cabin? His wife, Eva, questioned the decision from the beginning. Mark could have saved some grief by listening to her.

A close relative. If available, you might consult a retired parent, uncle, aunt, or cousin who knows you well and might guide or support your transition.

A close friend. An obvious potential adviser or sounding board is your best friend. Who better to ask about your future? For example, Pamela asked Wanda, her former college roommate, for advice about future careers.

Six Kinds of Role Models

1. Trailblazer—experienced expert
2. Mentor—personal, voluntary, one-to-one guidance
3. Teacher—specialist in helping people learn
4. Coach/counselor—paid mentor
5. Hero—historical or media personality
6. Adviser and sounding board—mate, friend, or relative

"Our relationship has finally marinated."

CHOOSING ROLE MODELS THAT FIT

As you seek the best role model(s) to guide your Next Phase, you might do these four steps:

Step 1: Consider your Social Style (Outgoing or Contemplative or Mixed)

In choosing role models, consider seeking out those who have *the same Social Style as yours* (see page 60). Among other things, you can see how role models with the same social needs have adapted their living situations and careers to make the kinds of social connections they (and you) prefer. If you interview your role model(s), ask about the fit with your shared Social Style. For example, William, who had an Outgoing style, chose Randy as his adviser, a good fit because Randy also has an Outgoing Social Style.

Step 2: *Clarify Your Goal*

Decide what you want from your role models. Here are some possibilities; more than one of these might apply—and you might have another purpose in mind:

- Help in understanding your personality or situation? (Example: William and Randy.)
- Assistance in identifying possible options? (Example: Charles and his son.)
- Help in choosing among options already identified? (Example: Pamela and Wanda.)
- Answers to specific questions about career experiences? (Example: Peter's interviews.)

Step 3: *Brainstorm Possible Role Models*

As you consider possible role models, try these questions as thought starters:

- Who were your childhood heroes?
- Who did you imitate in your family while growing up?
- What teachers did you like or admire at school?
- What characters did you find appealing in your favorite books?
- Who are your favorite public personalities (actors, athletes, authors, public figures)?
- What candidates for public office do you find inspiring?
- Whom in your workplace do/did you respect?
- What friend(s) or acquaintance(s) do you wish you could be more like?
- Whom among world leaders do you admire?
- Who influenced a significant choice in your life?
- What spiritual leader impresses you?
- In difficult times, whom did you ask for advice?

Step 4: Identify Key Qualities

Everyone seeks something different in a role model. For example, you might want a role model who has experience in a certain pursuit, like real estate, interior design, or poetry. Someone else may look for a role model who has insight and wisdom in handling emotional issues in relationships, or a sharp eye for finances and honesty in dealing with facts.

Key qualities to look for include *personal compatibility* and *complementary* personal traits. First, consider whether you want to seek a *compatible* role model similar to you—maybe someone who shares not only your Social Style, but also your Stress and Activity Styles. If you have a Contemplative Social Style, a Responsive Stress Style, and an Independent Activity Style, think about seeking a role model with those same traits. Finding a match on one or more of the personality traits can help you clarify your needs through your similar role model's experiences.

Consider whether you want a *complementary* role model in some areas. For example, you might look for someone who appears to have the Decision Style *opposite* your own, the one you find *least* comfortable. If you have an Empathetic style, you could look for someone astute at budgeting and problem solving. If you have an Analytic style, you might look for someone more compassionate who works well with people.

A complementary role model can prove especially helpful if you know you have an emotional blind spot. A role model can help illuminate your blind spot, through proficiency at a style you have trouble adopting when it's needed. One type of emotional blind spot involves a *personal strength overemphasized*, a habit of expressing a preference for one side of a trait in a variety of situations, without being aware that the habit sometimes doesn't fit. Put another way: when your only tool is a hammer, all problems become nails, even if they aren't!

Ron, the production manager, had a Structured Planning Style.

When Ron made a decision about something (like his early retirement), he closed the door to further input. He went ahead without the benefit he could have gained from reexamining the plan in light of new data (or the Flexible side of the trait pair).

INTERVIEWING A ROLE MODEL

Do you have a role model in mind? If he or she is alive and accessible, consider setting up an interview. You'll need to allow for plenty of lead time. Do something to make the experience fun and attractive, such as buying him or her lunch or a drink.

You might write out your questions in advance, and even send them ahead so the person has time to consider them. Then prepare to take notes. (You might even ask permission to make a tape recording.) Some sample questions appear on pages 174–175.

NOW REVISIT THE INGREDIENTS OF YOUR NEXT PHASE

Since you first met Laura, the stay-at-home mom, in chapter 2, she has made satisfying progress toward clarifying her Next Phase. After selecting the Ingredients of her Next Phase, Laura leaned toward starting a career in interior design. To learn more, she interviewed two interior designers and then decided to take some design workshops to gain more insight and understanding into the profession.

Whether or not Laura chooses a career in interior design after participating in the workshops, she will have benefited greatly from the experience. She wins either way. For example, if she finds out she likes interior design, she wins, because she has a head start on developing the skills she will need for the new career. If she finds out it is not for her, she still wins. Now she can eliminate that path after a modest investment of time and effort—and some education to show for it. (If you need to learn more, as Laura did, consider visiting more role models.)

After you interview your role models, go back and review the Ingredients of your Next Phase. Consider what you have learned from your role models and what questions remain. Take your time. Think about learning more before you commit to a particular course of action. After all, you have the rest of your life ahead of you!

If your role models have helped you clarify the Ingredients for your Next Phase, as they did for Peter and William, get ready to move forward, set your goals, and make your plans in the next chapter.

Sample Questions for Role Models Who Made Transitions to New Phases

1. What led you to the path you chose?
2. Looking back, what circumstances prompted you to consider a new phase?
3. What alternatives did you consider?
4. At what point did you finally make the decision to go the way you went?
5. Which features of the path you chose did you find most appealing?
6. What steps did you go through in planning your new phase?
7. Besides financial planning, what other kinds of planning did you do?
8. Did you take a vacation or recess between your earlier phase and your new one? How long?
9. As you began your Next Phase, what were your plans?
10. After the transition, what parts of your plans worked out about the way you expected?
11. What happened in starting your Next Phase that surprised you?
12. How did you adjust your plans as you went along?

13. How did you deal with unanticipated events?
14. What lessons did you learn from this transition that you would apply if you faced another transition?
15. Overall, how satisfied are you with your life since transition?
16. What do you enjoy the most about this new phase of your life?
17. What two things do you miss most from your life before?
18. If married, what has your spouse done differently, if anything, since you started your Next Phase?
19. Looking back, what if anything would you do differently?
20. What three pieces of advice would you give a friend facing a transition like yours?

Sample Questions for Role Models Who Did Not Make Transitions to New Phases

1. When did you first know that you had found the right path for you?
2. Which two or three of your personal qualities best prepared you for the path you've taken?
3. What do you like most about this pursuit?
4. What do you like least?
5. What did you have to learn, and what did you have to unlearn, to master this pursuit?
6. What was the most difficult adjustment you had to make?
7. What advice do you have for someone just starting out?
8. In today's world, what opportunities do you see that might not have existed when you started?
9. What obstacles do you see today?
10. If you were preparing now for this pursuit, what education or training would you seek?

CHAPTER 10

What Is Your Planning Style?

*How Understanding Your Planning Style Offers
the Final Key to a Fulfilling Retirement*

CARMEN'S DILEMMA

"Retiring will be delightful," Carmen said. "Why not? I won't have
to get to work at seven thirty in the morning. My time will be my
own, and there are so many exciting options!"

Even after teaching art in a private school for twenty years, Carmen, sixty-two, still has to make an effort to arrive on time. She
dislikes schedules and refuses to wear a wristwatch. She envisions
a new phase after retiring, with freedom to explore and enjoy all
that life has to offer—at her own pace.

Single, financially secure after her second marriage ended, and
living alone, Carmen feels ready to retire, and she imagines fantas-
tic possibilities. She could make the extra bedroom an art studio
and sell more paintings. Or maybe she could take that part-time
job designing floor displays at her friend's clothing store. She could
always get a job at the art supply store. Or perhaps she could get
a doctorate in art history. Carmen's options seemed endless: practice her jazz guitar and play evenings at the corner restaurant, join
the Peace Corps, go to Spain to visit Picasso's home, and maybe
make a pilgrimage walk across Spain. She's always wanted to learn

Spanish. Maybe she could take courses in Spanish art. So many wonderful choices!

When we asked Carmen to narrow to her Best Options, she got stuck when her list had twenty-two entries. She simply couldn't bring herself to eliminate more. "I have to keep my options open!" she exclaimed. "I can't close any more doors now, when I finally can choose . . ."

Carmen's strong Flexible Planning Style made it difficult to commit to one appealing option and bypass others. With effort many people who have this Planning Style make the tough choices and move ahead. Will Carmen narrow her options and choose? Or, like some with Flexible styles, will she remain torn among attractive choices, or add to her confusion by discovering more possibilities? Carmen could use some help from a friend, preferably one with a more Structured Planning Style, like Hugh.

HUGH'S DREAM

After working as a tax attorney most of his adult life, Hugh, sixty-four, dreamed of becoming a writer after retiring.

"Once I read the legal thrillers *The Firm* and *The Pelican Brief*, I knew I had to write," Hugh said. "I converted the sunroom in my Manhattan apartment into a writing studio. I planned my writing schedule for the first year. I made a list of agents to contact. I even outlined some plots I think will sell. I feel like the real deal!"

Unfortunately for Hugh's dream of becoming the next John Grisham, he soon realized that creative writing wouldn't fit his Outgoing, Interdependent personal style. Rather than finding himself excited to get into his (expensively renovated) new writing studio, he soon found himself dreading the isolation.

For a successful Next Phase, you do need a passion. However, as Hugh experienced, it has to fit your personality. You can find out the hard way, like Hugh. Or you can hold back from committing to any pursuit, like Carmen. Or you can plan and test-drive your future so you feel secure in the choices you're making. A test-drive consists of *a small trial or experiment with an unfamiliar pursuit to get a realistic preview without making a major commitment.*

Hugh's rude awakening came from overusing his Structured Planning Style. In his eagerness to organize his life, common for those with Structured styles, he locked down early on a course of action and planned without further input. He had his mind made up. Unfortunately, that approach doesn't work well in planning for retirement. Hugh needed a more open, Flexible Planning Style, opposite his preference. After his jarring failure, we urged him to take time to understand his Planning Style.

This last Personality Quiz of the book, about your Planning Style (page 180), has obvious relevance for planning a new phase. Your Planning Style is also obvious to people around you. Whether you like your life organized and scheduled, as Hugh does, or more open and flexible like Carmen, or a little of both, those who know you will notice. Your friends may appreciate your organization or your spontaneity—as long as you don't overdo it.

UNDERSTANDING YOUR PLANNING STYLE

Before you plan your Next Phase, it helps to become aware of your Planning Style, as both a strength and a blind spot. First consider it as a strength.

Planning Style as a Strength

For Hugh, the lawyer, a Structured Planning Style helps organize his work. His To-Do lists help him plan his tasks for the day, week, and month. He schedules his time carefully to manage his cases, meetings, and commitments with ease.

Carmen, the art teacher, has the opposite strength: spontaneous and open, ready to go with the flow, Carmen can seize the moment. Carmen's easygoing approach works well in preparing art lessons and working with students. She enjoys the variety of possibilities in teaching art. She tolerates the weekday work schedule as long as she can keep her weekends and summers open to enjoy what life brings.

Flexible Planning Style: *Strengths.* If you have a Flexible style, your relaxed approach enables you to improvise on a moment's notice. You handle unexpected events and last-minute changes with grace and ease. Under pressure of a deadline, you might come up with a brilliant, spontaneous solution.

Structured Planning Style: *Strengths.* If you have a Structured style, planning comes easily; you tend to enjoy it, do it well, and find comfort in the organization you create. You prepare in advance and follow through. People can depend on you.

Mixed Structured/Flexible Planning Style: *Strengths.* While you're comfortable making plans, you don't overplan or get too attached to an agenda. You can make a new one as needed. You adjust your plans to deal with the unexpected. You roll with new turns of events, and adapt or rethink your plans as you go.

PERSONALITY QUIZ #7: WHAT IS YOUR PLANNING STYLE? STRUCTURED VS. FLEXIBLE

Consider how you think, feel, and act *most of the time* when away from work and free to be yourself. Mark each statement *true* or *false*. If a statement is sometimes true and other times false, mark it *true* if it describes you even *slightly* more often than not. Avoid responses based on your work role or what others expect or how you'd like to be. If in doubt, go with your *first reaction* or *intuition*.

True	False	
❑	❑	1. If I do a task that's not on my To-Do list, I might add it so I can cross it off.
❑	❑	2. I like to have specific goals and a schedule so I can stay focused.
❑	❑	3. I do much better at following a careful plan than winging it.
❑	❑	4. Before starting a project, I like to list the steps.
❑	❑	5. Friends and coworkers appreciate my organization.
❑	❑	6. I get annoyed when people want to change the plan at the last minute.
❑	❑	7. I have specific places for most things I own, and I try to keep them there.
❑	❑	8. Before starting any new venture, I need a solid plan.
❑	❑	9. Ordinarily I don't like surprises.
❑	❑	10. I prefer to have decisions settled as soon as possible.

_____ My total score (count the number of boxes marked *true*)

What Your Score Means

A score from 7, 8, 9, or 10 indicates a Structured Planning Style—the higher the score, the more consistent your preference. *A score of 4, 5, or 6 indicates a Mixed Structured/ Flexible Planning Style. A score of 0, 1, 2, or 3 shows a Flexible Planning Style*—the lower the score, the more consistent your preference.

Structured Planning Style (7–10): You like to live in an organized and orderly way. You prefer to plan and avoid surprises. You go step-by-step and prefer closure and structure. You tend to like things settled—and once you've decided, you dislike reopening the decision. Comfortable with rules, you appreciate conscientiousness and reliability in others. You tend to reach conclusions quickly, and try not to leave your plans open-ended. Spontaneity does not come easily or naturally.

Mixed Structured/Flexible Planning Style (4–6): You feel equally at ease with a spontaneous or a planned approach to life. Sometimes you like rules and guidelines, other times they get in the way. You may alternate between open-ended and organized styles, or try to integrate them by planning in a Flexible way. Friends may see you as balanced, unpredictable, or both.

Flexible Planning Style (0–3): Flexible and adaptable, you like to keep your options open, seize the moment, and try not to let plans get in the way. You feel restricted by rules. You prefer to go at your own pace and exploit new opportunities that arise. At ease with ambiguity and happy to be surprised, you appreciate originality and nonconformity in others. Spontaneity comes more easily than planning. You may have difficulty deciding on a course of action—and if you do decide, you may want to reconsider your decision at the last minute.

Your Personality Profile

Record your Planning Style (Structured, Mixed, or Flexible)—the seventh trait on your Personality Profile on page 185.

Now that you have identified your Planning Style, you have a complete Personality Profile—all seven of the key traits for a successful Next Phase. This last quiz gave you the final piece of information you need to know about yourself before planning your Next Phase.

Take Time to Redefine Roles at Home

Life changes in many ways at retirement. You and your mate could spend more time at home together. If so you'll need new rules and roles. We recommend sitting down together and writing out new job descriptions before you retire. Discuss household chores (who does what?), the budget, how you'll use the rooms, and how much alone time you need. Redefining your roles is critical if one member of the couple has managed the household. If time together with your mate at home will change, better talk about it now.

Recognize Your Planning Blind Spot

You have a planning blind spot if you prefer one Planning Style so strongly that you have trouble using the opposite style, or if you use your preferred Planning Style when the situation calls for the opposite (like the carpenter whose only tool is a hammer).

The Structured Bear Trap The bear trap develops if you have a Structured Planning Style and overdo it by snapping shut on a decision too early. The trap shuts too soon when researching a new idea or looking at options—closing off input before finding out enough to make informed decisions. "No more information, thanks; I made up my mind," you might say, as Hugh did. He created an expensive writing studio for a career that didn't fit. In this blind spot, you could fail at retirement on the first try, too, like Hugh.

The Flexible Juggler If you carry the Flexible style to the extreme, you could become the juggler. "I need my options open; I have to have opportunities," you say. Then, overwhelmed with possibilities, you might cry, "If I choose one I have to let the others go—and I can't let any of them go . . ." As the comic-strip character Pogo once said, "We are overwhelmed with infinite possibilities." Carmen had the same issue.

If you do have this blind spot, you may hesitate to commit to a specific course of action. You might have trouble making any decision at all, like Carmen. If all the doors are open, it's tough to hear opportunity knocking at any of them!

Ambivalent If you have a Mixed Structured/Flexible style, your blind spot is ambivalence—between exploring and planning, or between staying open to new input and setting an agenda for action. When you can use both the Flexible and Structured Planning Styles with equal comfort, you might get stuck between them. The result? Reluctant to commit, but hesitant to further explore—which door?

YOUR PERSONALITY PROFILE

When you finished the seventh Personality Quiz, you had the result needed to complete your Personality Profile (page 185). If you've recorded your Planning Style (Structured, Mixed, or Flexible) and your results from it and the other six quizzes, it's done. To add results now from of any of the seven quizzes, you'll find

Opportunity Knocking?

their pages listed below. (You might use a highlighter to mark your seven personal traits.)

Seven Personality Quizzes	Page
#1, Social Style	60
#2, Stress Style	72
#3, Activity Style	94
#4, Information Style	114
#5, Outlook Style	134
#6, Decision Style	162
#7, Planning Style	180

MY NEXT PHASE PERSONALITY REVIEW

Don't fail at retirement on your first try for lack of self-understanding. Take a moment to review your seven key personality traits. Refer to your complete Personality Profile, page 185, for your record of your traits.

My Personality Profile

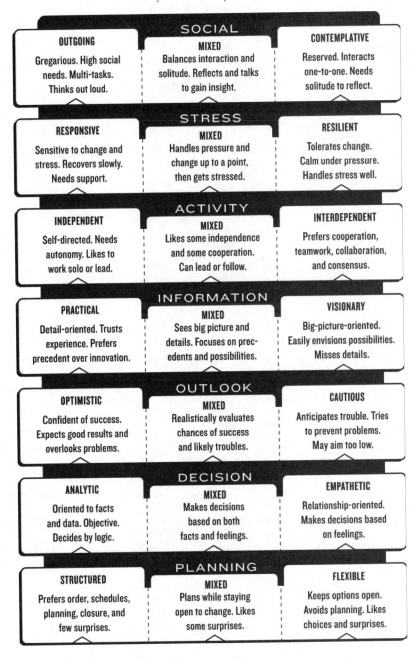

SOCIAL

OUTGOING	MIXED	CONTEMPLATIVE
Gregarious. High social needs. Multi-tasks. Thinks out loud.	Balances interaction and solitude. Reflects and talks to gain insight.	Reserved. Interacts one-to-one. Needs solitude to reflect.

STRESS

RESPONSIVE	MIXED	RESILIENT
Sensitive to change and stress. Recovers slowly. Needs support.	Handles pressure and change up to a point, then gets stressed.	Tolerates change. Calm under pressure. Handles stress well.

ACTIVITY

INDEPENDENT	MIXED	INTERDEPENDENT
Self-directed. Needs autonomy. Likes to work solo or lead.	Likes some independence and some cooperation. Can lead or follow.	Prefers cooperation, teamwork, collaboration, and consensus.

INFORMATION

PRACTICAL	MIXED	VISIONARY
Detail-oriented. Trusts experience. Prefers precedent over innovation.	Sees big picture and details. Focuses on precedents and possibilities.	Big-picture-oriented. Easily envisions possibilities. Misses details.

OUTLOOK

OPTIMISTIC	MIXED	CAUTIOUS
Confident of success. Expects good results and overlooks problems.	Realistically evaluates chances of success and likely troubles.	Anticipates trouble. Tries to prevent problems. May aim too low.

DECISION

ANALYTIC	MIXED	EMPATHETIC
Oriented to facts and data. Objective. Decides by logic.	Makes decisions based on both facts and feelings.	Relationship-oriented. Makes decisions based on feelings.

PLANNING

STRUCTURED	MIXED	FLEXIBLE
Prefers order, schedules, planning, closure, and few surprises.	Plans while staying open to change. Likes some surprises.	Keeps options open. Avoids planning. Likes choices and surprises.

1. What Are Your Social Needs?

Review—Social Style: Outgoing, Contemplative, or Mixed (quiz #1, page 60)

- How much companionship and face-to-face interaction do you need? Do you want social connection and companionship through your days with little or no time alone (Outgoing)? Periods of solitude plus some one-to-one connection (Contemplative)? Or all of these (Mixed)?
- Do the Ingredients for your Next Phase meet your needs for social connection and solitude?

2. What Is Your Stress Reaction?

Review—Stress Style: Responsive, Resilient, or Mixed (quiz #2, page 72).

- How do you deal with stress? Does your personal mirror tend to minimize problems (Resilient), magnify life's demands (Responsive), or show them the actual size (Mixed)?
- Do you have to take care to avoid getting overwhelmed (Responsive) or overextended (Resilient), or to locate your stress threshold (Mixed)?
- Do you know how much stress to expect from life change? Are you ready to manage it?

3. How Much Autonomy Do You Need?

Review—Activity Style: Interdependent, Independent, or Mixed (quiz #3, page 94)

- How much autonomy do you want to direct your activities or those of others (Independent)? How much cooperative activity and teamwork do you need (Interdependent)? Do you need an equal blend of solo and collaborative activity (Mixed)?

- Does your Next Phase have the mix of solo and team pursuits for the fulfillment you want? Enough independent accomplishment? Collaboration? Other sources of fulfillment you enjoyed in your career?

4. What Is Your Information Style?

Review—Information Style: Practical, Visionary, or Mixed (quiz #4, page 114)

- Do you first see the forest or a tree? Precedent or possibility?
- Consider how your Information Style influenced the possible options you listed for your future.

5. What Is Your Outlook Style?

Review—Outlook Style: Optimistic, Cautious, or Mixed (quiz #5, page 134)

- Do you see the glass half full (Optimistic) and look past trouble, or see it half empty (Cautious) and overlook benefits, or sometimes see it half full and sometimes half empty (Mixed)?
- Did you consider how your Outlook Style influenced the way you selected the ingredients for your Next Phase?

6. What Is Your Decision Style?

Review—Decision Style: Analytic, Empathetic, or Mixed (quiz #6, page 162).

- Do you have an emotional blind spot in making decisions about your Next Phase more from the heart (Empathetic) or head (Analytic), or possibly an ambivalent mix?

- Did you consider how your Decision Style influenced your choices about your role models or your list of ingredients for your Next Phase?

7. *What Is Your Planning Blind Spot?*

Review—Planning Style: Structured, Flexible, or Mixed (quiz #7, page 180).

- How do you turn your planning strength into weakness? Do you overdo your Structured style by planning too fast (bear trap)? Overdo your Flexible style and can't choose (juggler)? Or get stuck in ambivalence between exploring and planning (Mixed style)?
- Do you need help from a role model or friend to choose so you can plan, or stay open and explore further before choosing and making a plan?

READY TO PLAN YOUR NEXT PHASE?

Our goal in this book is to help you effectively plan a Next Phase that fits your personality. The quizzes tell you your personality traits. You've discovered what brings fulfillment to your life. You've brainstormed options, identified the Ingredients of your future, named your Next Phase, and perhaps selected one or more role models to guide you.

Now it's time to make your plan and prepare to test-drive your future. Here is a preview of the six steps:

1. Add the Ingredients (page 153)
2. Set your goals, from three choices: continue, expand, or test-drive
3. Plan your test-drive(s)
4. Do a financial reality check
5. Do a personal reality check (write a letter to yourself)

6. Schedule your recess (pure time-out before your Next Phase)

We've given you a completed sample Planning Template showing Laura's Next Phase (pages 190–191). Look at this example to see how Laura filled in the Ingredients of her Next Phase, before filling in your own template.

LAURA'S PLANNING TEMPLATE

Laura filled in her list of Ingredients onto her planning template in nine categories: Health/Exercise, Challenging Pursuit/Passion, Relationship with Mate/Life Partner, Friendship, Family, Self-Development/Spirituality, Fun/Enjoyment, Home/House/Residence, and Community. Laura crossed out *Spirituality*. You can see the result in her template. Some Ingredients clearly fit into more than one category. Laura decided to take up tennis, and it seemed like exercise, friendship (with her friend Louise), and fun. We suggested that she include it in all three places.

As shown in Laura's example, each item on the template has one of three simple goals: Continue (marked "C"), Expand ("E"), or Test-drive ("T"). Laura had only one item marked E for Expand—her "weekends with John." She wondered about the goal of shrinking an activity, like maybe phasing out the school board. We suggested putting "continue" if she'll keep on doing it; maybe later it drops off.

PLANNING TEMPLATE
Laura's Next Phase

Goal = Continue (C) *Expand* (E) *Test-Drive* (T)

HEALTH / EXERCISE

- Morning walks (C)
- Tennis twice weekly (T)

CHALLENGING PURSUIT / PASSION

- Career as interior designer, part-time (T)
- Get training and join the local Interior Design Association (T)
- Continue leading political action committee (C)

RELATIONSHIP WITH MATE / LIFE PARTNER

- "Weekends" together (John's time off) (E)
- Travel to John's layover destinations (T)

FRIENDSHIP

- Tennis with Louise (T)
- Annual Summer Solstice Open House (C)
- Lunches with friends (C)

FAMILY

- Visits with children between semesters (C)
- Family summer vacations (C)
- Sister time (C)

SELF-DEVELOPMENT / ~~SPIRITUALITY~~

• Reading and college courses on interior design (T)
• Seminars in interior decorating (T)

FUN / ENJOYMENT

• "Weekends" with John (E)
• Visit children (C)
• Tennis with Louise (T)
• Sister time (C)
• Political action committee (C)
• Home renovations (C)

HOME / HOUSE / RESIDENCE

• Home renovation and interior decorating projects (C)
• New home office (T)

COMMUNITY

• Political action committee (C)
• School advisory committee (C)

OTHER

RECESS

• "Hawaii Getaway" - March 2nd to 24th

SIX STEPS TO COMPLETE YOUR PLANNING TEMPLATE

You'll find your personal Planning Template—like Laura's, only blank—on page 192. To complete it, you'll need the list you made of Ingredients of your Next Phase, page 153. You may discover that you've left out a key ingredient, like an annual event you intend to continue (Laura remembered her annual summer solstice open house). If so, you can just add it to your template.

Use the following six steps as you complete your Planning Template. If you need more space than the pages provide, copy the template onto a separate sheet of paper.

Step 1: Add the Ingredients

Using the list of Ingredients you created earlier, write each item where it goes in the template. It's okay to list one Ingredient in multiple categories; that can help you see each life domain more clearly.

Step 2: Set Your Goals

Before you set goals, consider your Planning Style (Structured, Flexible, or Mixed). If you have a Structured style, you'll probably find it easy to set specific goals. Just don't overdo. Push yourself to keep it simple. For each pursuit choose one of these three goals: continue (write "C" next to it); expand (write "E"); or test-drive ("T"). Consider adding a numerical target only if you need one to feel comfortable. Leave at least a few open-ended.

If you have a Flexible Planning Style, you might feel yourself resisting the idea of setting goals. It's okay. Go only as far as you feel comfortable. But consider pushing yourself a little to set a few comfortably uncomfortable goals. Lean into your zone of discomfort, to develop the skill you find difficult. It will help you now, and later when you run into another situation that calls for goal setting and planning—if you're not already used to stretching in this way.

Especially now, on the threshold of a new phase, you owe it to yourself to pay attention to the sides of your personality with which you're least comfortable. Lean into your discomfort, like a basketball player learning to dribble with the opposite hand to manage situations that can be handled only that way. If you're Optimistic, practice the Cautious outlook; if you're Cautious, practice optimism.

Step 3: Plan Your Test-Drives

We recommend that you test-drive any new, unfamiliar activity. After you've consulted role models to find out how to do a safe test-drive, learn firsthand whether the activity is compatible with your personality. You can find out from experience if it offers the fulfillment you want from it.

If your test-drive confirms that your new pursuit fits your personality, you win! You have a better idea how to succeed at it; you already have a start. If your test-drive shows a misfit, you still win, because you limited your commitment to a learning trial. A failed test-drive is a learning experience, and better than a failed retirement. You can rethink the new pursuit with the benefit of your new knowledge.

In Laura's case, her test-drive called for a realistic preview of a possible new career as an interior designer. Fortunately she was able to approach and learn from two role models, friends Jane and Larry, both interior designers. They helped her arrive at these next steps for her career plan:

- Join the local Interior Design Association and go to the monthly meetings.
- Start taking evening courses on interior design at the community college.
- Participate in the Interior Decorating and Design Workshop in Chicago, in July.

- Shadow Jane (career interior designer) for two days in May. (*Shadowing* means following a person closely through the whole workday.)
- Set up a temporary home office in the back bedroom, and try working alone there for a half day at a time with just the phone (Laura's stretch goal).

Laura also planned for test-drives that included:

- Travel to meet John for five-day visits in Seattle (May) and Paris (August)
- Meet Louise for tennis, Wednesday mornings at eight a.m. (April)
- Start weekly tennis lessons in April

Now plan your test-drives. Figure out and write down in your calendar your next steps for all Ingredients showing the goal test-drive. Having them in your calendar lets you check to be sure you do all of them—and, if necessary, push some of them off to later dates.

Step 4: Do a Financial Reality Check—Visit Your Financial Planner

Now that you have nearly completed your planning template for your Next Phase (all but the Recess), you can do the crucial financial check. You know what you want to do. Share your plans with your financial planner (or review your financial situation yourself). Can you find the income you need? Will you need income from earnings to close any gaps? Must you rethink any pursuits to afford or finance them?

For example, Carmen loves French art. When she finally completed her planning template, it included travel to France. After reviewing her plans with her financial adviser, though, Carmen found out she needed to adjust. She chose to travel to Montreal, a less expensive destination for French art. In addition, she decided to work in a local art gallery two days a week to generate some earnings, and gained the privilege of showing some of her own work there. The additional earnings fund her travels. As a member of the art community, she has made contacts that open doors when she does travel. In one of our TeleClasses, Carmen said, "If I hadn't worked through the finances of my plan I never would have come up with these alternatives. My financial adviser really responded when I showed her the template with all the specifics."

We suggest you follow Carmen's example. If you have limited financial resources, having a plan that fits your personality becomes even more critical in discovering ways to find fulfillment in your Next Phase.

Step 5: Do a Personal Reality Check—Write a Letter to Yourself

Next, as a personal reality check, please write a letter to yourself. First, decide how long you want to wait to see how your Next Phase is going. Three months? Six? Flexible Laura opted to check after six months. Someone with a more Structured Planning Style might want monthly checks.

What about you? Select a date and write this in your calendar: "Read letter from self." Next, take a sheet of paper and write a note to yourself about judging the success of your Next Phase in general, and your test-drives in particular. Ask questions like these:

- Have I found fulfillment?
- Do I have enough companionship and one-to-one time?
- Do I have enough time alone?
- Do I have some unscheduled time? Enough time structure?
- Do I have opportunities for cooperation with others? Enough autonomy?

Consider a few more specific questions about test-drives:

PLANNING TEMPLATE
My Next Phase
Goal = Continue (C) *Expand* (E) *Test-Drive* (T)

HEALTH / EXERCISE

CHALLENGING PURSUIT / PASSION

RELATIONSHIP WITH MATE / LIFE PARTNER

FRIENDSHIP

FAMILY

SELF-DEVELOPMENT / SPIRITUALITY

FUN / ENJOYMENT

HOME / HOUSE / RESIDENCE

COMMUNITY

OTHER

RECESS

- Did you manage the weekly walk with George (or other test-drive)?
- Did you enjoy the class on interior decorating (or other test-drive)?
- How did the visit(s) with (people) to (destination) go?

After writing down the questions, seal the letter in the envelope, and put it where you'll know to find it later.

Step 6: Schedule Your Recess

In our seminars some people have what we call "vacation confusion." They think of retirement as well-deserved rest, and confuse retirement with an extended vacation. Once you've rested up, then what?

So take a vacation when you retire. Get your well-deserved rest. Wait to start your Next Phase when you return from your recess. Come back rested, stronger, and ready to *reengage* with life. Be sure to figure the cost of Recess in your financial plan.

One of our models of success, George, a member of the board of directors of a Seattle nonprofit organization, offers this advice: "Before starting what you'll do next, take time to unplug. Give yourself some pure downtime—a few weeks or a month or more, with no pressure. Decompress. Make a gentle passage from the life you're leaving."

About five years ago, George's company unexpectedly eliminated his job. He took it hard and got depressed. His wife insisted that they take advantage of the open calendar to spend the month in Greece that they'd promised themselves. "But before we leave," she told George, "I want you to know what you're doing when we get back."

George made the reservations for travel in two weeks. Then he did some soul-searching and talking with people about his options for retirement. "When we left for our month in Greece, I knew exactly what I'd do when we got back. The month in Greece gave me the downtime I needed to let go and move on."

We've heard this advice about a recess from many successful retirees. It applies to anyone starting a new endeavor in life. If you don't have a recess as one of the Ingredients of your Next Phase, please add it now. If your transition is years away, write in what you imagine you'll prefer when the time comes. You can revise later.

Think of your recess as a quiet passage or a pause between one phase and the next, perhaps a rewarding vacation between graduation and your first job. Know in advance what you'll do the morning after you return.

You don't have to leave your home for your recess. Time-out is a state of mind. As Emily Dickinson demonstrated, you can travel far in your imagination while staying at home. Some people use their recesses for renovation projects or just to catch up on books, movies, and rest. Some finish their test-drives before they go on recess; others wait until afterward. Laura chose a Hawaii getaway as her recess and decided to do test-drives afterward. What choices will you make?

TEST-DRIVE YOUR FUTURE

Do you feel confident knowing what you'll do in your Next Phase? Do you understand yourself well enough to know that your new phase fits your personality and includes the sources of fulfillment you want to carry forward from your career? If so, this book has done its job. Here's to your Next Phase—we hope you've found your best retirement!

RESOURCES

Sections in quotation marks are taken verbatim from the Web site indicated. (Visit Retirement Resources at www.MyNextPhase.com for a continuously updated list. If you see a resource we missed, please e-mail us at Info@MyNextPhase.com.)

COMMUNITY AND FRIENDSHIP

- **CatholicMatch**—"Provide[s] single Catholics with a place to meet others and discern their vocation. We realize that God calls people to the religious and single life as well. Catholic-Match.com has brought people together for marriage, helped others towards the priesthood and religious life, and given those leading a single life the opportunity to deepen an understanding of that calling." www.catholicmatch.com
- **CatholicSingles**—"Find fellowship, love and a lasting relationship with others matching your profile and faith." www.catholic singles.com
- **Empty Nest Moms**—A community of female empty nesters. www.emptynestmoms.com
- **Eons**—All about celebrating life that begins at fifty. www.eons.com
- **Fitness Singles**—An "online dating community for sports and fitness enthusiasts." www.fitness-singles.com

- **Green Singles**—"Personal ads for progressive singles in the environmental, vegetarian, and animal rights community and other green singles who love the outdoors, holistic living, personal growth and spirituality—a place to meet and network for friendship, dating, romance and the exchange of information and ideas." www.greensingles.com
- **Grandparents & Grandchildren Camp**—Fosters "understanding, care and respect for nature, people and their critical interdependence" (for grandparents and grandchildren—no parents permitted). www.sagamore.org
- **JDate**—"An ideal online destination for Jewish men and women to find friends, dates, and even soul mates, all within the faith." www.jdate.com
- **Jmatch**—A Jewish dating service. www.jmatch.com
- **Over Fifties**—Bulletin board and chat room for people over fifty. www.overfifties.com
- **Red Hat Society**—"Welcome to the place where there is fun after fifty (and before) for women of all walks of life. We believe silliness is the comedy relief of life and, since we are all in it together, we might as well join red-gloved hands and go for the gusto together. Underneath the frivolity, we share a bond of affection, forged by common life experiences and a genuine enthusiasm for wherever life takes us next." www.redhatsociety.com
- **The Right Stuff**—"An international introduction network for single graduates and faculty of a select group of excellent universities and colleges. It is a civilized, manageable and affordable way to meet well-educated members of the opposite sex." www.rightstuffdating.com
- **Senior Friend Finder**—Seniors looking for friends, romance, and fun. www.SeniorFriendFinder.com
- **The Transition Network**—"TTN is a vibrant community of more than twenty-five hundred women, predominantly from the New York City area, who are facing transitions by dynami-

cally taking control of their lives. Most members are in their fifties and sixties and represent a spectrum of professions in business, government, health care, academia, not-for-profits, and the arts." http://www.thetransitionnetwork.org

- **Women in Our Sixties**—Meeting place for only women sixty or older. http://home.teleport.com/%7Elionne/sixty.html

VOLUNTEERING AND SERVICE

- **Action without Borders**—"Connects people, organizations and resources to help build a world where all people can live free and dignified lives." www.idealist.org
- **Amizade**—"Encourages intercultural exploration and understanding through community-driven volunteer programs and service-learning programs. Amizade Volunteer Programs offer a rewarding combination of exploration, service and understanding in communities around the world." www.amizade.org
- **Big Brothers Big Sisters** –"Mission is to help children reach their potential through professionally supported, one-to-one relationships with measurable impact." www.bbbsa.org
- **Cross-Cultural Solutions**—A recognized leader in the international volunteer field, sending thousands of volunteers overseas every year. www.crossculturalsolutions.org
- **Experience Corps**—Offers new adventures in service for Americans over fifty-five. Works to solve serious social problems, beginning with literacy. www.experiencecorps.org
- **Experience Works**—"Improve[s] the lives of older people through employment, community service and training. Experience Works has grown to be the nation's leading provider of training, employment, and community service for low-income older people." www.experienceworks.org
- **Generations United**—Mission is "to improve the lives of children, youth, and older people through intergenerational

collaboration, public policies, and programs for the enduring benefit of all." www.gu.org

- **Global Volunteers**—Facilitates short-term service opportunities on community-development programs in host communities abroad. Mobilizes service-learning teams year around to work in eighteen countries on six continents. www.globalvolunteers.org

- **Habitat for Humanity International**—A nonprofit, nondenominational Christian housing organization at work in every state of the United States and in one hundred other countries around the world. www.habitat.org

- **Junior Achievement**—Uses hands-on experiences to help young people understand the economics of life. In partnership with business and educators, brings the real world to students, opening their minds to their potential. www.ja.org

- **The Senior Corps**—A national network of projects that place older people in volunteer assignments in their communities. www.joinseniorservice.org

- **United Way**—Provides links to the organizations supported by United Way that need volunteers. www.national.unitedway.org

- **Virtual Volunteer**—Lets you volunteer from "virtually" anywhere—so you can contribute your time and expertise without ever leaving your office or home. www.volunteermatch.org/virtual/

- **VolunteerMatch**—"Brings thousands of good people and good causes together. Find a cause that needs your help and let your inner beauty shine." Nice feature is that you can enter your zip code, interest, and availability. www.volunteerrmatch.org

FAMILY

- **Ancestry Library**—A collection of family history how-to and genealogy learning materials on the Internet. www.ancestry.com

- **Ellisisland**—Port of New York passenger record genealogy search. www.ellisisland.org
- **Rootsweb**—"The oldest and largest free genealogy site." www.rootsweb.com

HEALTH

- **Breast Cancer Assessment**—"An interactive tool designed by scientists at the National Cancer Institute (NCI) and the National Surgical Adjuvant Breast and Bowel Project (NSABP) to estimate a woman's risk of developing invasive breast cancer." www.cancer.gov/bcrisktool
- **Care Pathways**—"Created and maintained by Registered Nurses (RNs) dedicated to providing seniors and their families access to quality information, products and services." www.carepathways.com
- **Department of Health and Human Services Administration on Aging**—Provides information on a number of health-related issues for seniors. www.aoa.dhhs.gov
- **Real Age**—The biological age of your body, based on how well you maintain it. www.realage.com
- **Your Disease Risk**—"The source on prevention. Here, you can find out your risk of developing five of the most important diseases in the United States and get personalized tips for preventing them. Developed over the past ten years by the Harvard Center for Cancer Prevention, Your Disease Risk collects the latest scientific evidence on disease risk factors into one easy-to-use tool." www.yourdiseaserisk.harvard.edu/english

HOME

- **Best Places**—Resource for the best places to retire. www.bestplaces.net
- **Cruise Ship Condos** www.residensea.com

- **Digsville**—A home-exchange club with listings in more than fifty-five countries. www.digsville.com
- **Find Your Spot**—A short quiz to help you find the best place for you to live. www.findyourspot.com
- **4homeex**—A global network for home exchange. www.4homex .com
- **Freehomeawayfromhome**—Offers a large listing of home-exchange sites with free membership. www.freehomeaway fromhome.com
- **Holswap**—This site's two services—Holiday Home Exchange and Swap Vacations Worldwide—offer home exchanges and vacation rentals in privately owned villas. www.holswap.com
- **Homeexchange**—Provides "The vacation alternative where two families agree to swap homes for a vacation." www.home exchange.com
- **Ihen**—The International Home Exchange Network was the first Web site devoted to listing home exchanges and private rentals. www.ihen.com
- **RCI**—Pioneered the concept of vacation exchange and time-share resell. www.rci.com
- **Tug2**—A self-help community of time-share owners. www.tug2 .net
- **Vacation Exchange Network**—Provides its members, vacation owners from around the world, with comprehensive exchange services and time-share resell. www.intervalworld.com

TRAVEL

- **Active Journeys**—Specializes in organizing active holidays worldwide. "Walking, cycling, rafting, sea kayaking, and canoeing affords you the time to smell the fragrances, absorb the sights and sounds, all the while taking in the beauty of the country and wilderness around you." www.activejourneys.com
- **Activity Ireland**—Has been in operation since 1989 and

provides a number of Adventure Travel options in Ireland. www.activity-ireland.com

- **Adventure Directory**—A portal to almost every kind of adventure. www.adventuredirectory.com
- **Adventure for Women**—Adventure travel designed especially for women. www.adventurewomen.com
- **American Hiking Society**—"The only national organization dedicated to promoting and protecting America's hiking trails, the natural areas that surround them, and the hiking experience itself." www.americanhiking.org
- **Canadian Voyageur Adventures**—Provides guided canoe excursions in replica fur trade canoes. www.gocanoe.com
- **Culinary College Directory**—A portal of comprehensive directories of culinary, travel, and hospitality programs on the Internet. www.patanegra.net
- **Dante Alighieri—Siena**—School offers a wide range of Italian language courses, Italian cultural courses, culinary courses, opera courses, and drama courses for all age groups and all levels of Italian. www.dantealighieri.com
- **Earthwatch Institute**—Supports scientific field research by offering volunteers the opportunity to join research teams around the world. This unique model is creating a systematic change in how the public views science and its role in environmental sustainability. www.earthwatch.org
- **Educational Cruises** www.classicalcruises.com
- **Evert Tennis Academy (Tennis Camp)**—Offers an adult clinic. www.evertacademy.com
- **Expedia**—A leading Internet travel site. www.expedia.com
- **Geographic Expeditions**—A pioneer of travel to remote and challenging destinations since 1982. Offers a varied portfolio of overland tours, treks, walks, and expeditionary voyages to the world's most astonishing places. www.geoex.com
- **Grandkids and Me Foundation**—Under the umbrella of the National Heritage Foundation, helps build strong families

through intergenerational relationships. www.grandkidsand
me.com

- **Grandtravel**—"Developed by a team of teachers, psychologists, and leisure counselors, it is dedicated to helping grandparents create lasting memories for themselves and their grandchildren." www.grandtrvl.com

- **Grown Up Camps**—The Internet's most comprehensive directory of traditional, sports and fantasy camps, recreational activities, and educational vacations for the adult traveler. www.grownupcamps.com

- **Grizzly Bear Adventure Tours**—At Knight Inlet Lodge in beautiful British Columbia, Canada, enjoy one of the premier grizzly bear viewing spots in the world, set amid the dramatic snowcapped peaks of Canada's rugged coastline. www.grizzlytours.com

- **Holland America**—A leading provider of premium cruises. Activities and destinations cater to the preferences of adults. www.holland/america.com

- **The International Kitchen**—Dedicated to offering the best of Italian and French lifestyle and cuisine. The International Kitchen now offers more than seventy unique trips. www.theinternationalkitchen.com

- **The John Newcombe Tennis Ranch (Tennis Camp)**—Offers adult tennis packages designed to ensure maximum enjoyment and improvement of your game, no matter what your existing level of play. www.newktennis.com/tennis_adultprograms.html

- **La Varenne**—Founded by Anne Willan in 1975, this famous French cooking school directs its culinary programs at the Château du Feÿ in Burgundy, France. www.lavarenne.com

- **Myths and Mountains**—Offers journeys inside a country's culture in Asia, Africa, Southeast Asia, South America, and Antarctica. www.mythsandmountains.com

- **Orbitz**—A leading online travel company. www.orbitz.com

- **Princess Cruises**—Offers a variety of destinations intended to appeal to adults. www.princess.com
- **Richard Petty Driving Experience**—"Get behind the wheel or Ride-Along in a NASCAR-style stock car at more than twenty locations. Have the experience of driving or riding in a stock car at some of the most famous racing facilities in the world." www.1800bepetty.com
- **Senior Exchange**—"The Only Home Exchange Exclusively for the Over 50 Age Group." www.seniorshomeexchange.com
- **Sherpa Expeditions**—"Founded thirty years ago, long before adventure travel became as widely accepted as it is today, and long before the Internet. Professional tour operators rather than an Internet travel site." www.sherpaexpeditions.com
- **Spanish Steps**—Features walks across Spain following the pilgrimage route known as the Camino de Santiago. Also offers a number of Adventure Walking tours in Italy, Argentina, France, and Portugal. www.spanishsteps.com
- **Travelocity**—A leading Internet travel site. www.travelocity.com

SPIRITUALITY

- **Belief Net**—"We are a multi-faith e-community designed to help you meet your own religious and spiritual needs—in an interesting, captivating and engaging way. We are independent. We are not affiliated with a particular religion or spiritual movement. We are not out to convert you to a particular approach, but rather to help you find your own. Fundamental to our mission is a deep respect for a wide variety of faiths and traditions." www.beliefnet.org
- **John Templeton Foundation**—"The mission of the John Templeton Foundation is to pursue new insights at the boundary between theology and science through a rigorous, open-minded and empirically focused methodology, drawing together tal-

ented representatives from a wide spectrum of fields of expertise." www.templeton.org

- **2nd Half Strategies**—"Our purpose is to inspire people to create their legacies with intention, passion, and their innate spiritual wisdom." www.2ndhalfstrategies.com

SELF-DEVELOPMENT: LEARNING AND EDUCATION

- **AARP**—"A nonprofit, nonpartisan membership organization for people age 50 and over. AARP is dedicated to enhancing quality of life for all as we age. We lead positive social change and deliver value to members through information, advocacy and service. AARP also provides a wide range of unique benefits, special products, and services for our members." www.aarp.org
- **Boston Center for Adult Education**—"Seeks to provide educational opportunities for adults that foster personal and professional development, enhance a sense of community, and encourage social responsibility." www.bcae.org
- **Colorado Free University**—Colorado's premier continuing-education resource. www.freeu.com
- **Distance Grad Schools**—"An online resource for graduate-school information with more than fifty-eight thousand programs listed." www.distance.gradschools.com
- **Elderhostel**—"A not-for-profit organization dedicated to providing extraordinary learning adventures for people 55 and over." www.elderhostel.org
- **Gen Plus USA**—"Brings meaning, respect and resources to you, the plus generation, aged 50 and older, in the USA and Canada." www.genplususa.com
- **Get Educated**—An online counseling center for adult learners seeking accredited online college degrees. www.geteducated. com
- **The Learning Annex**—Provides students with the tools they need to change careers, make more money, improve their rela-

tionships, empower their lives, and support personal and spiritual growth. www.learningannex.com

- **Mature Resources**—"A free national ezine and business directory. We specialize in enriching the lives and needs of Baby Boomers through Seniors." www.matureresources.org
- **Maturity Works**—"The National Council on the Aging is a national network of organizations and individuals dedicated to improving the health and independence of older persons and increasing their continuing contributions to communities, society and future generations." www.maturityworks.org
- **Mentor**—"A trusted voice for the power of mentoring. We work to ensure that every child who wants and needs a mentor has the right one." www.mentoring.org
- **Osher Life Long Institute (OLLI) at Echerd College**—"Classes and programs are designed for everyone age 50 or better." www.eckerd.edu/olli
- **Petersons**—"Connects individuals, educational institutions, and corporations through its critically acclaimed books, Web sites, online products, and admissions services." www.petersons.com
- **Phoenix University Online**—"Beginning in the early 1970s, University of Phoenix reinvented the way in which working adults could achieve a higher education and made academic innovation, quality, and accountability its hallmark. It pioneered an educational and service model specifically geared toward the way adults learn best and made its programs widely available to working students by using commonsense scheduling and fresh new approaches to academic delivery." www.phoenix.edu
- **Senior Journal**—"Senior Citizens News and Information Daily on the Web." www.seniorjournal.com
- **Study Abroad Links**—"Provides an easy-to-use and practical starting point for anyone who is looking for information and resources to assist them in selecting a school, program or tour for study abroad or educational travel." www.studyabroadlinks.com

- **The Teaching Company**—"Brings engaging professors into your home or car on DVD, audio CD and other formats." www .teach12.com
- **Third Age**—"An online media and direct marketing company focused exclusively on serving the needs of midlife adults." www.thirdage.com
- **2 Young 2 Retire**—"Help[s] you navigate the uncharted waters of longevity." www.2young2retire.com
- **The University of the Third Age (U3A)**—A highly successful adult-education movement providing opportunities for older adults to enjoy a range of activities associated with well-being in later life. www.worldu3a.org

MENTAL CHALLENGE

- **American Contract Bridge League**—Promotes the fun and challenge of bridge and supports educational and playing opportunities for bridge enthusiasts throughout North America. www.acbl.org
- **Count on Sudoku**—Play a new game every day online. www .counton.org/sudoku
- **Flying Colors Art Workshops**—Specializes in organizing and hosting art workshops around the world, including the USA, Europe, Latin America, and Asia. www.flyingcolorsart.com
- **Internet Chess Club**—A loosely organized community of Internet chess players. www.chessclub.com
- **ItsYourTurn.com**—Offers a number of Internet games for free. Games available include chess, backgammon, Jamble (a word game), checkers, Battleboats, Pente, Go, and Stack4. More than sixty different games and variations. www.itsyourturn.com
- **OK Bridge**—"The friendliest, best-run online bridge club in the world. Play bridge anytime, anywhere." www.okbridge.com
- **Older Adult Service (OASIS)**—"A national nonprofit educational organization designed to enhance the quality of life for

mature adults. Offering challenging programs in the arts, humanities, wellness, technology, and volunteer service, creates opportunities for older adults to continue their personal growth and provide meaningful service to the community." www.oasis net.org

- **Sudoku Game**—Offers a new game every day online. www .sudokugame.com
- **Web Sudoku**—A Sudoku site on the Internet. http://play.web sudoku.com

WORK SUPPORT

- **Biz Planit**—"Assists in business planning and raising capital." www.bizplanit.com
- **Bizstarters**—"One-stop source of all help needed to plan and launch a really terrific new business at 50 and beyond." www .bizstarters.com
- **Career Builder**—Combines presence in more than 130 local newspapers and the Internet for job searches. www.career builder.com
- **Creative Retirement**—"A collection of articles, retirement tips, interesting places to visit, and fun things to do." www .creativeretirement.org
- **Dream Jobs to Go**—Offers information about a wide range of types of jobs. www.dreamjobstogo.com
- **Experience Works**—"A national, nonprofit organization that offers training, employment, and community service opportunities for mature workers." www.experienceworks.org
- **Go 60**—"Older workers' employment opportunities. Helping seniors improve with age." www.go60.com
- **Job Hunters Bible**—Created by the author of *What Color Is Your Parachute?* www.jobhuntersbible.com
- **Monster**—Internet site for job searches. www.monster.com
- **The National Business Incubation Association**—"The world's

leading organization advancing business incubation and entrepreneurship." www.nbia.org

- **Retirement Jobs**—"Our goal is to identify companies most suited to older workers and match them with active, productive, conscientious, mature adults seeking a job or project that matches their lifestyle." www.retirementjobs.com

- **SCORE (Service Corps of Retired Executives)**—"Provides professional guidance and information, accessible to all, to maximize the success of America's existing and emerging small businesses." www.score.org

- **Seniors for Hire**—"A nationwide online Career Center for U.S. job seekers 50 and over to find job openings from businesses that value a diverse workforce and actively recruit and hire older workers, retirees and/or senior citizens." www.seniors 4hire.org

- **Senior Job Bank**—Free to over-fifty job seekers. Completely confidential service matching job seekers with employers and good jobs. www.seniorjobbank.com

- **Senior Jobs**—"A job placement service that matches companies and job seekers age 50 and above in the Northern Virginia suburbs of Washington, D.C." www.seniorjobs.org

- **Seniors Jobs**—"Over 50" career site, serving the employment needs of the "Third Age." www.seniorsjobs.com

- **Working Solo**—"The information source for independent entrepreneurs and companies serving the SOHO (Small Office/ Home Office) market." www.workingsolo.com

REFERENCES AND RESEARCH

The scientific studies and findings referenced in *My Next Phase* are listed below by chapter.

CHAPTER 1: ARE YOU READY TO RETIRE?

Gawande, A. The way we age now: Medicine has increased the ranks of the elderly. Can it make old age any easier? *The New Yorker*, April 30, 2007: 50–59.

Franco, O. H., et al. Effects of physical activity on life expectancy with cardiovascular disease. *Archives of Internal Medicine*, 2005: 165(20): 2355–60.

Weuve, J., Kang, J. H., Manson, J. E., et al. Physical activity, including walking, and cognitive function in older women. *The Journal of the American Medical Association*, 2004:2006: 1(1): e52 292(12): 1454–61.

De la Fuente-Fernandez, R. Impact of neuroprotection on incidence of Alzheimer's disease. *PLoS ONE*, 2006: 1(1):e52.

Thompson, R. G., Moulin, C. J., Hayre, S., and Jones, R. W. Music enhances category fluency in healthy older adults and Alzheimer's disease patients. *Experimental Aging Research*, 2005: 31(1):91–9.

Barnes, L. L., Mendes de Leon, C. F., Wilson, R. S., et al. Social resources and cognitive decline in a population of older African Americans and whites. *Neurology,* 2004: 63(12): 2322–6.

Erickson, E., Erikson, J. M., and Kivnick, H. Q. *Vital Involvement in Old Age.* New York: Norton, 1994.

House, J. Social isolation kills but how and why? *Psychosomatic Medicine* 2001: 57B(3): 212–22.

Fratiglioni, L., Paillard-Borg, S., and Winblad, B. An active and socially integrated lifestyle in late life might protect against dementia. *Lancet Neurology,* 2004: 3(6): 343–53.

Perspectives for the Media on Longevity with World Experts on Population Aging. April 5–8, 2002, Madrid, Spain. International Longevity Center in New York. www.ilcusa.org/_lib/pdf/madrid2002.pdf.

Vaillant, G. E., DiRago, A. C., and Mukamal, K. Natural history of male psychological health, XV: retirement satisfaction. *American Journal of Psychiatry,* 2006: 163(4): 682–8.

Siegrist, J., vondem Knesebeck, O., and Pollack, C. E. Social productivity and well-being of older people: a sociological exploration. *Social Theory & Health,* 2004: 2(1): 1–17.

CHAPTER 2: IS RETIREMENT HISTORY?

Social Security Online: www.ssa.gov/historyage65.html.

Costa, D. *The Evolution of Retirement: An American Economic History, 1880–1990* (National Bureau of Economic Research Series on Long-Term Factors in Economic Development). Chicago: University of Chicago Press, 1998: 7.

What Older Workers Want from Work. AARP poll: www.aarp.org/states/az/az-news/a2004-04-20-olderworkers.html.

Dychtwald, K. *Age Wave.* New York: Bantam Books, 1990.

Employment Policy Foundation, The American Workplace 2003: Realities, Challenges and Opportunities, Washington, D.C., August 27, 2003. www.epf.org/news/nrelease.asp?nrid=179.

American Association of Retired People (AARP): www.aarp
.org.

Farber, H. What do we know about job loss in the United States?
Evidence from the Displaced Workers Survey, 1984–2004.
Economic Perspectives, 2005:13–28.

Munnell, A. H., Sass, S., Soto, M., and Zhivan, N. Do
older workers face greater risk of displacement? Center for Retirement Research at Boston College. www.bc
.edu/centers/crr/issues/ib_53.pdf.

Bender, K. A., and Jivan, N. A. What makes retirees happy? Issue in
Brief 28. Chestnut Hill, MA: Center for Retirement Research
at Boston College, 2005.

World Demographic Trends—report published December 2004
by the Economic and Social Council of the United States.
www.un-ngls.org/World%20demographic%20trends%20
-%20N0463983.pdf.

Erikson, E. H. *Dimensions of a New Identity*. New York: Norton,
1974.

Bender, K. The well-being of retirees: evidence using subjective
data. Center for Retirement Research at Boston College. No-
vember 2004. www.bc.edu/centers/crr/papers/wp_2004-24.pdf.

Current Population Reports. Projections of the Number of House-
holds and Families in the United States: 1995 to 2010. www
.census.gov/prod/1/pop/p25-1129.pdf.

CHAPTER 5: WHAT IS YOUR STRESS STYLE?

American Heart Association: Put a Spring in Your Step—Add Exercise to Your Daily Routine. www.americanheart.org/presenter
.jhtml?identifier=3029685.

Gallo, W. T., Bradley, E. H., Siegel, M., et al. Health effects of
involuntary job loss among older workers: Findings from the
health and retirement survey. *The Journals of Gerontology Series
B: Psychological and Social Sciences*, 2000: 55(3): S131–40.

Gallo, W. T., Teng, H. M., and Falba, T. A., et al. The impact of late career job loss on myocardial infarction and stroke: a 10-year follow up using the health and retirement survey. *Occupational and Environmental Medicine*, 2006: 63(10):683–7.

Wilson, R. S., Arnold, S. E., Schniede, J. A., et al. Chronic psychological distress and risk of Alzheimer's disease in old age. *Neuroepidemiology*, 2006: 27(3):143–53.

Phillips, A. C., Carroll, D., Evans, P., et al. Stressful life events are associated with low secretion rates of immunoglobulin A in saliva in the middle-aged and elderly. *Brain Behavior and Immunity*, 2006: 20(2): 191–7.

Ong, A. D., Bergeman, C. S., Bisconti, T. L., and Wallace, K. A. Psychological resilience, positive emotions, and successful adaptation to stress in later life. *Journal of Personality and Social Psychology*, 2006: 91(4): 730–49.

Lee-Baggley, D., Preece, M., and Delongis, M. Coping with interpersonal stress: role of the big five traits. *Journal of Personality*, 2005:73(5): 1141–80.

Thoits, P., and Thoits, A. Stress, coping and social support processes: Where are we? What's next? *Journal of Health and Social Behavior*, 1995: 35, extra issue: 53–79.

Galvin, J. A., Benson, H., Deckro, G. R., Fricchione, G. L., and Dusek, J. A. The relaxation response: reducing stress and improving cognition in healthy aging adults. *Complementary Therapies in Clinical Practice*, 2006: 12(3): 186–91.

Benson, H., and Klipper, M. Z. *The Relaxation Response*. New York: HarperCollins, 2000.

Shetty, R. C. Meditation and its implications in nonpharmacological management of stress-related emotions and cognitions. *Medical Hypotheses*, 2006: 65(6):1198–9.

Bandura, A. *Self-Efficacy: The Exercise of Control*. New York: W. H. Freeman, 1997.

Miller, J. G. Information input, overload, and psychopathology. *American Journal of Psychiatry*, 1960:116: 695–704.

CHAPTER 8: WHAT IS YOUR OUTLOOK STYLE?

Covey, S. R. *The 7 Habits of Highly Effective People*. New York: Simon & Schuster, 1989.

Rosenthal, R. Covert communication in classrooms, clinics, courtrooms, and cubicles. *American Psychologist*, 2002:57(11): 839–49.

CHAPTER 10: WHAT IS YOUR PLANNING STYLE?

Locke, E. A., and Latham, G. P. Building a practically useful theory of goal-setting and task motivation: A 35-year odyssey. *American Psychologist*, 2002:57: 705–17.

Covey, S. R. *The 7 Habits of Highly Effective People*. New York: Simon & Schuster, 1989, 95.

INDEX